# THE
# F.A. BOOK
# OF
# SOCCER

An Official Publication of
The Football Association

WILLIAM HEINEMANN LTD
*Official Publishers to The Football Association*

*Distributed by*
PAN BOOKS LTD, 18–21 CAVAYE PLACE, LONDON SW10 9PG

William Heinemann Ltd
15 Queen St, Mayfair, London W1X 8BE
LONDON  MELBOURNE  TORONTO
JOHANNESBURG  AUCKLAND
First published 1975

SBN 0 330 24470 1 (Pan)
SBN 434 25014 7 (Heinemann)

Printed and bound in Great Britain
by Morrison & Gibb Ltd,
London and Edinburgh

# CONTENTS

Design by M. Mohan

# THE NEW STRIKERS

## by Brian Glanville
### Sunday Times Association Football correspondent

When England were eliminated from the 1974 World Cup, the first time they had failed to reach the Finals, it was largely because they could not score goals. They could not score goals because they had not the strikers to score them, the players capable, in the fetching Italian expression, of 'inventing the game'.

Had Gerd Muller been on the field that night against Poland at Wembley, there would have been no two ways about it; England's sheer pressure, instead of being ultimately counter-productive, exposing them to the quick breakaway, would have brought all the goals they required. But there was no Muller, and the packed Polish defence, with its brave, erratic, lucky goalkeeper, gave away just one penalty; and that a dubious one.

It was said of the extraordinary Muller, by a jealous German girl athlete, that all he did was stand in the penalty-area and score goals, while his colleagues did all the work. One might as well say that all Newton did was sit under an apple tree and discover the Force of Gravity; that all Michelangelo did was hack away at blocks of stone.

What Muller has done has been perfectly remarkable. In a period when we have been told, and shown, that goals have never been so difficult, he has contrived to set record after record, wiping out in a few short years that which Uwe Seeler, with the national team, took twelve years to establish, getting more than anybody in the 1970 World Cup, winning games galore for Bayern Munich, at every level.

In a sense, Muller defies analysis. He is a roly poly figure, very thick in the thighs, whom Zlatko Cjaicowski, Bayern's former Yugoslav manager, would not have signed at all had his directors not overruled him; a player who can virtually disappear from a game for long periods, contributes little yet will suddenly

Gerhard Muller, described by Brian Glanville as 'perfectly remarkable'.

Pietro Anastasi, a centre-forward who 'can do all things down the left wing', seen here tackling Derby's Archie Gemmil.

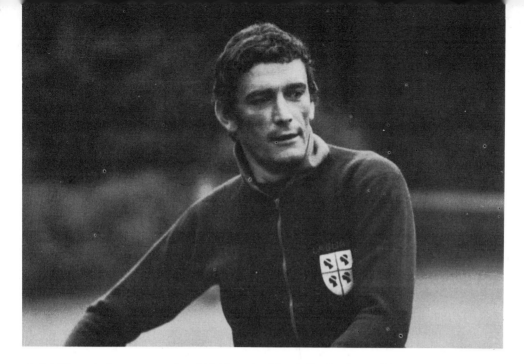

Luigi Riva, the 'most coveted and highly valued footballer in the world'.

come to life, virtually materialize, in and around the goal area. Some of his goals are almost bizarre in their execution; that gentle little back header, for example, with which he defeated the excellent goalkeeper, Piot, to score against Belgium in the 1972 semi-final of the Nations' Cup, in Antwerp. He can shoot and volley splendidly with either foot, but what he has above all is the divine gift of knowing where to be when the ball comes over.

Pelé has been around for a great deal longer than Muller, but when he was still only 17, he showed, in Sweden, that he was a master of the half chance, the opportunity created out of nothing. I still look back with relish on the goal he scored against the Swedes themselves in the World Cup Final of 1958, on that rainy afternoon in Stockholm. Calmly and serenely, though he was only 17 years old, he caught the ball on his thigh in a crowded Swedish penalty-area, hooked it over his head, and volleyed ferociously home. One could go on almost indefinitely cataloguing Pelé's marvellous goals. I shall confine myself to one more, that which he scored in Guadalajara against Rumania in Brazil's first World Cup match of 1970. Coolly catching a fine, long pass from Gerson on his chest, he pivoted to shoot past Raducanu.

Pelé, of course, was a much more gifted, versatile, all-round player than Muller, but he shares the stocky German's gift for being uncannily in the right place at the right time; and for making time his own, creating for himself space and

9

opportunity, where a lesser forward would find none.

There is, however, another kind of modern striker, almost as effective in his way, who has been bred particularly in Italy, but is very seldom to be found in Britain. This sort of player is the consequence, the by-product, of obsessionally defensive football, such as is played in the Italian League, where *catenaccio* is king, and man-to-man marking the relentless rule.

He is not just a centre-forward, like Martin Chivers, or just a striking inside-forward, like Mick Channon or Allan Clarke. He is not limited to attacking from any one specific position, whether down the left, down the right, or through the middle. He is enormously resourceful, as he has to be when he has an opponent forever breathing down his neck, and a sweeper charging in at him if he succeeds in shaking that opponent off. He can hold and shield the ball superbly until help, like the American cavalry, arrives. He is perfectly capable and willing to take on two or three men at a time.

In a word, he is a Super Striker, whose apotheosis may be found in Gigi Riva, the most coveted and highly-valued footballer in the world, an ex left-winger with a marvellous left foot who likes, however, the middle of the attack to be his preserve. Pietro Anastasi, for five years the game's most expensive footballer, is

Jimmy Greaves, 'wonderfully skilled and effective . . .'

George Best, 'all the qualities of the great striker . . .'

another, a centre-forward who can do all the things down the touchline which a classical left-winger could once do.

Beyond Italy, one thinks of the marvellous Johann Cruyff, who first made a great team out of Ajax, and since then has made a fine one out of Barcelona; a centre-forward whose finest work has so often been done down the left, and whose immense quickness and courage in the penalty-area, not to mention his heading, has brought him so many goals.

Very few British players have attained such heights, in such categories. There was Jimmy Greaves, wonderfully skilled and effective near goal, a great sprinter, too, in his early youth, but never, like Muller, a success in a World Cup. There was George Best, who has shown all the qualities of the great striker, whether of the Muller or Riva kind.

But these, alas, are the exceptions which prove the rule.

11

# FOOTBALLER OF THE YEAR

## by Dennis Signy
### Secretary of the Football Writers' Association since 1966

Stanley Matthews, Tom Finney, and Danny Blanchflower merit the use of that over-rated word in soccer – great. Sir Stan, the idol of Blackpool and the Potteries, not forgetting England; Tom Finney, the Preston plumber who was questionably the greatest sportsman to put on football boots; and Danny Blanchflower, the erudite Irishman who led and talked Tottenham to the coveted League-Cup 'double' in the early 1960s, have something else in common. They are the only players to have twice won the coveted Footballer of the Year trophy.

Just as the F.A. Cup is the daddy of all knockout competitions, so is the Footballer of the Year aloof from all imitators. Since members of the Football Writers' Association decided in 1948 to organize the annual award, their choice – beginning with Matthews – has been *the* Footballer of the Year. You can nominate your Player of the Month, or Player of the Week – it will soon be Player of Saturday afternoon 2 p.m. kick off games! – but the annual get-together of the Football Writers' and their guests at a West End of London function two days before the F.A. Cup-Final to acclaim the Footballer of the Year is special.

In my years as secretary of the F.W.A. I have had the pleasant task of breaking the news of their selection as Footballer of the Year to such fine modern players as Billy Bremner – surely a candidate to join Matthews, Finney, and Blanchflower as a second-time winner – the Charlton brothers, George Best, Dave Mackay, Tony Book, Frank McLintock, Gordon Banks, Pat Jennings and Ian Callaghan.

I do know incidentally that Bremner collected over 90 per cent of the votes in 1969–70, the most convincing win in the quarter of a century since the soccer writers put up a statuette.

The 1968–69 result when Mackay and Book finished equal for the honour was

12

the first and only tie. It's a little-known secret that a vote arrived for Book in the next post at my home after the result had been declared.

Mackay, like Blanchflower an inspiration behind Tottenham's 'double' success in the 1960's, was only one vote adrift on a previous occasion – when Matthews won the honour for the second time in 1962–63. Many thought that Mackay should have won the award then, but the Soccer Writers showed, perhaps, an unexpected sentimental streak in returning Matthews, then in the twilight of a magnificent career.

Mackay was pipped for the title by the odd vote . . . but the runner-up is rarely remembered. The Footballer of the Year stands supreme.

What makes a Footballer of the Year? My colleagues of the immediate post-war era thought in terms of sportsmanship and image in their deliberations and few could fault their early choices on either score. The names roll off the tongue, as if from the pages of a Debrett of Soccer – Matthews; gentleman Johnny Carey the only winner from Eire; dear old Joe Mercer; the late Harry Johnston; England's long-serving skipper, Billy Wright; Nat Lofthouse, and Finney.

There are some 225 members of the F.W.A. today. Early in the New Year full members get their ballot forms and nominate their choice of Footballer of the Year. The closing date for votes is generally the Monday after the F.A. Cup semi-finals and, if there has been a criticism over the years, it has been that the eventual winner is often in the Wembley line-up.

Johnny Carey, only winner from Eire, collected the coveted trophy in 1948–49.

Two immortals of football who won the Footballer of the Year award. *Above* Stanley Matthews and *below* Tom Finney.

I contend that the true test of a choice for Footballer of the Year is how he stands up to the passing of time. Banks, Best, the Charltons – fans will look back 10 years from now and speak with equal reverence of them and their feats as the older generation do of Matthews, Finney, and Blanchflower. Don Revie, today the most successful manager in English football, won the award in 1954–55. Moore, who eventually succeeded Wright as England's skipper, won it in 1963–64.

Of course, there are great players who have *not* won the coveted award. Johnny Haynes was perhaps hampered by being with Fulham – Denis Law and Jimmy Greaves are other modern greats who have not been in the reckoning. I am sure each reader could nominate a dozen favourite players worthy of the title, but I defy you to say that any of the 24 winners did not merit recognition at the time and that most do not stand up well to the test of time.

One of the most popular choices was Bert Trautmann, Manchester City's German-born goalkeeper. He and Jimmy Adamson, currently Burnley's manager, are the only non-internationals in the list since 1948. Goalies are a rarity. Between Trautmann's selection in the mid-1960s the men in jerseys did not get a look in until Gordon Banks won it three years ago, and Pat Jennings followed in 1973.

Dave Mackay and Tony Book were linked in a unique tie for the F.W.A. award in 1968–69.

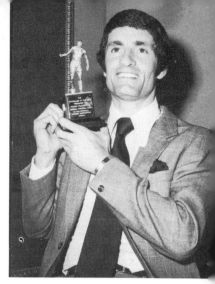

Nat Lofthouse (1952–53), Jimmy Adamson (1961–62), and Frank McLintock (1970–71).

All the previous Footballers of the Year are invited to the annual dinner, traditionally held at the Café Royal in London until a growing demand for tickets meant a switch to a larger venue three years ago. Last year's dinner, at the Blooms-bury Centre Hotel, was attended by 778 guests. Soccer's top brass from the F.A. and the Football League mingled with managers, players, and soccer writers from all corners of England, Ireland, and Wales.

When the choice of player is determined it is my job to notify him and his Manager – and this sometimes poses problems. I rang Ken Friar, the Arsenal secretary, to find out where Frank McLintock would be in the morning as the team were en route to West Bromwich. Ken obviously alerted Frank to my possible call, and the *Sunday Times* referred in mocking terms to 'an inspired leak'.

I also remember Brian Clough's reaction when I told him that Dave Mackay, who was favourite for the title, had shared it with Tony Book. 'Go back and count the votes again', said Cloughie.

The best speech ever made by a Footballer of the Year was that made by Jackie Charlton. He was so good that we invited him back in 1973 as a guest speaker. I won't tell who made the worst speech – it's a matter of opinion anyway – or reveal the player who upset a few people by turning up late and minus a tie to collect his award.

The Footballer of the Year dinner is a football family occasion. One of the highlights of the year for me is getting the top table guests in the V.I.P. room before the dinner and hearing Joe Mercer and Billy Wright swapping stories or Danny Blanchflower and Tom Finney in serious football conversation. When he sees and hears a quartet such as that the current Footballer of the Year is entitled to feel he has deserved the highest accolade of the soccer writers.

16

# EQUIPPED TO SURVIVE

Terence Delaney describes
the rare football
talents of
MIKE CHANNON

Mick Channon, of Southampton and England, is a lean, curly-haired, cheerful young man, a dangerous and devoted goalscorer, and one of the most exciting attacking footballers in the game. With so much emphasis nowadays on highly-organized defence, life is hard for strikers. Openings are well-covered, chances are few and gone in a flash, defenders are hard and determined men. One can understand the impulse in any player, unless he is the big, solid, ruthless type himself, to move the ball on quickly, stay in the open, and avoid the crunches.

Mr McMenemy rates him very highly indeed. 'He's simply the best player in England,' he says. 'He has pace, skill, and courage – the three qualities you look for when you're thinking of signing a young player. You often find two of them, rarely all three together.'

Channon loves football, and goals, too much to hold off from the heart of the

Mike Channon slams one at goal in the match against Argentina at Wembley.

action. His stride is long and limber, his acceleration remarkable, and he reckons he has as good a chance as anyone to reach the ball first. When he has it, he holds it tight, shields it, and turns with it well under control in the most crowded situations. With defenders moving in on him, his loose, dodgy movement leaves him ready to feint, switch his direction, and be off again, still perfectly balanced. Characteristically, he often chooses to head straight for the narrow space between them – the dangerous way. If it comes off, he's through, closing on goal, or well placed to switch a pass back into the middle. If not, he's likely to finish rolling on the ground, caught in the sandwich, or tripped after the ball has gone by an exasperated opponent who realizes too late he has lost touch with him.

'He gets to the bye-line more often than anyone,' the Southampton manager, Lawrie McMenemy, says. 'If he took all the chances he made himself, he'd break every goal record ever set.'

Channon takes a lot of punishment. One Saturday, when he was having a four-inch gash on his shin treated, one could see bruise-marks from earlier games all over him, from shoulders to toe. 'It's all part of the occupation,' Channon says. 'It's no good losing your temper about it. I'm an easy-going person – nothing really bothers me.' What about the temptation to retaliate? He laughs at that. 'I couldn't kick anyone if I wanted to. And if I put my fist up, they'd flatten me.'

Channon hasn't any particular advice to give to ambitious youngsters. 'If they

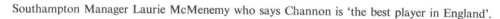

Southampton Manager Laurie McMenemy who says Channon is 'the best player in England'.

Channon extricates himself from a tight spot against Tottenham. John **Pratt** lunges for the ball.

want to play, they'll play at all costs,' he says. 'And if they're like I was, they wouldn't listen to anyone else.'

Channon is fit – the way he plays he has to be – but keep-fit exercises don't interest him. 'What he likes,' Mr McMenemy says, 'is competitive training with a ball. The rest bores him.' 'Of course,' Mr McMenemy points out, 'that's part of the main business of a manager – to vary the training routines so that players *don't* get bored.'

Another reason why Channon stays in good condition is that he is not one for the bright lights. He had a chance of a transfer to Tottenham, but doesn't regret letting it go. He's ambitious enough, but it would have meant giving up the country life that's so important to him when he's not playing. 'I love the country, and I've got a great home life,' he says. 'I enjoy going home, and I must have a private life to relax and get a bit of peace.'

Home now, after nine years with Southampton, is a new £30,000 house at Bishop's Waltham, and his passions, away from football, are horses and shooting. His racehorse Cathy Jane, now out at stud, was trained locally and won him nearly £5,000 in prize money, including the Brown Jack Stakes at Ascot. 'The country's great,' he says, 'people are genuine there, and say what they mean. When we lived in town, it was always kids at the door after autographs. I'll sign for anyone, but when I'm not playing I just want to be like everyone else.'

Channon's father was a foreman with the War Department at Larkhill, so the boy grew up right in the middle of Salisbury Plain, where there was nothing to do except play football, and dream of becoming a professional with Southampton or Swindon Town, the teams he and his father used to watch on Saturdays. When he was 15, and playing for Amesbury Secondary Modern School, his first ambition was realized. Ted Bates, the Southampton manager who had already discovered Terry Paine and Martin Chivers, arrived at the house one Sunday morning and signed him as an associate schoolboy.

The other realized dreams slotted into place – regular in the Southampton first team, England Under-23, full International cap. Logically, the next step would have been the World Cup Finals – but to Channon, as to many others, that was the big disappointment.

The result of the England-Poland match at Wembley nearly broke his heart, he says, 'but we were beaten fairly and squarely'. He's so full of vitality and the enjoyment of life that one suspects the heart is already healed. Now he's thinking of the Nations' Cup next year, and being in the England team that beats Scotland in the Home Internationals.

Mick Channon has an enviable temperament. 'A man so unpredictable on the field is bound to be a bit unpredictable off it,' his manager says, 'but he's no prima donna.' He is a spontaneous, natural player. He has his worries from time to time, but he shakes them off. If he's out of form, or misses a few penalties: 'I lose a bit of sleep, but I soon get over it. You're concerned, naturally, but you've got to have confidence. That's what you need to get out of trouble.'

He is an attractive, lucky man, and, in a hard profession, equipped to be a survivor.

Marvin Hinton of Chelsea beaten to the ball by Mike Channon.

# MANAGEMENT BY CONSENT

The England Team Manager, DON REVIE, talks
about his way of winning the respect of his players

During my career as Leeds United's manager, I received a number of offers from
other clubs. I turned them all down. I remembered that on signing apprentice
professionals I had always told them: 'If you show 100 per cent loyalty to me, I
will show 100 per cent loyalty to you.' All of which helps explain why I remained
at Leeds so long, and the very special relationship that existed between the players
and myself.

I got very close to the players. Indeed, without wishing to appear trite, I looked
upon them almost as sons.

Each Thursday, after training, we'd give them a soap and water massage, which I attended to myself. If a player's wife was celebrating a birthday or anniversary, I'd send her a box of chocolates or bunch of flowers.

In other words, I tried to instill a family atmosphere into the club and, to some extent, I have approached the job of managing the England team in the same way.

Loyalty and respect seem old-fashioned words nowadays, but, as far as professional football is concerned, these are still the most important qualities of all in my view. No manager could have asked for more loyalty and respect than the Leeds players gave me.

When Bill Nicholson quit as Tottenham's manager, he said he had found it increasingly difficult to handle players. 'There has been less respect from the players,' he said, 'and no manager can work without that.' Arsenal's manager Bertie Mee then went on record as saying: 'The permissive society has given us young footballers totally concerned with what they can get rather than what they ought to be giving.'

The day after Leeds United won the 1973–74 First Division League Championship Don Revie led his players in singing 'It's a grand team to play for . . .'

Maybe I was lucky, because the experiences which Nicholson and Mee have had in their dealings with players contrast sharply with mine. During my thirteen and a half years as Leeds United's manager, there was not one occasion when we came into conflict over their contracts. Indeed, they generally signed *blank* contracts. They would give me an idea of the financial terms they required, and then leave it to me to negotiate the best terms I could with the directors and fill in the details!

One problem common to all managers of successful clubs concerns the difficulty of maintaining their appetite for success. When Malcolm Allison left Manchester City for Crystal Palace, I remember him saying: 'You can be at a club too long. After a while, there's nothing new you can say to the players to help stimulate them.' Celtic's Jock Stein, one of my closest friends in football, has often echoed these sentiments when I've been in his company.

I've got to be honest and say that this was my biggest headache during my latter years at Leeds. It is only human nature for players to become a bit lackadaisical after a run of success and there were times when I, like Allison, feared that I had lost the knack of lifting the Leeds stars.

There were several ways in which the coaching staff and myself overcame this problem. During team talks, I frequently mentioned world-class golfers such as Arnold Palmer, Jack Nicklaus, and Gary Player, making the point that these performers, despite their immense wealth, remained as determined to achieve honours as when they started their careers.

Before the start of a season, the Leeds players were given specific targets. Prior to the 1968–69 campaign, for example, I told them: 'I want you to try and go through the season without losing a single League match.' Then, after a defeat at Manchester City, they set their sights on beating the record of four League defeats in a season, held by Arsenal. Leeds, in fact, equalled that record and, of course, won the Championship that season for the first time.

Manchester United's Sir Matt Busby once gave me an invaluable piece of advice on the manager's job when he told me: 'Never rock the boat.' What he meant is that it is essential for a manager to adopt a philosophical attitude towards setbacks, and keep the odd below-par performance by his team in perspective.

It can be very frustrating to see the many hours of hard work which the team and yourself have put in during the week suddenly wasted by a silly mistake on Saturday afternoon. I have always had a fierce will-to-win and tended to be rather intolerant of players' mistakes during my early days as Leeds manager.

I well remember a Second Division match at Rotherham in which Jack Charlton

24

made a mistake which caused Leeds to lose 2–1. I fired on all cylinders at Jack in the dressing room afterwards and a bitter slanging match developed. It culminated in us walking towards each other with clenched fists, and the other players had to hold us back!

I was completely to blame for that incident. Due to inexperience, I had allowed myself to lose my head . . . and it could so easily have caused a serious rift between the players and myself. Since then, I have usually saved any criticism of a player's performance until a few days after the match, when we've all had a chance to cool down and look at things objectively.

There's only one thing I demand from players, win, lose or draw, and that's 100 per cent effort. I got it from Leeds United's players – and so far I have got it from England's players, too.

Don Revie, as England team manager, faces photographers with England captain Emlyn Hughes.

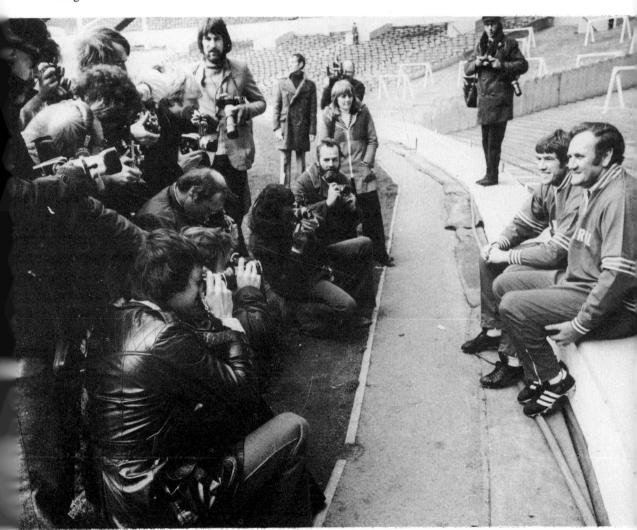

# GO SOUTH, YOUNG MAN!

### says Gordon McQueen,
Leeds United's Kilbirnie-born star.

Go South young man! That's my advice to any Scot back home who is keen to improve his game and I should know because I made that move myself.

Take it from me there is a big difference between English and Scottish league soccer and the set-up South of that border is just fine. When I joined Leeds from St Mirren in September 1972 I really felt the pinch in training. Everything was done at break-neck speed. After the leisurely atmosphere at Love Street, St Mirren, it was sheer murder, I can tell you!

It didn't take me long to adapt to the new jet-pace way and I soon began to reap the benefits of the rigorous routines we went through daily. That rough introduction to the English First Division opened my eyes in double quick time and made me understand why so many Scots players struggled when they first came South. It wasn't just the training either that was a class above anything in Scottish soccer. The coaches too, seemed to know their trade better than any I had come up against in Scotland.

Maybe that's a little unfair though. I mean I had moved to Leeds United and everybody knows well enough that they have demanded the best in all things for quite some time. Their coaching staff leave nothing to chance. Before every game we are all given a comprehensive run-down of our next opponents, and when I say comprehensive I'm not kidding. They told us every detail, so that when the game came around there was virtually nothing you didn't know about the guy you were marking. About the only thing we didn't know was his favourite colour or shoe-size.

That sort of painstaking preparation was new to me. Up at St Mirren we were told to go out and enjoy ourselves. It was as simple as that and I suppose a bit more of the Leeds professionalism would not have gone amiss.

Another aspect of the Southern game that was different from the game I had known before my transfer was that in England everything was more competitive. Training and practice games were all deadly serious. The players competed as if their lives depended on it.

At first I was a bit puzzled, but I soon realized that the First Division was not played for laughs and there was a serious attitude as far as the competition for first-team places went. That meant no holds barred when it came to training and I didn't need telling twice before I got stuck in with the rest of the lads.

Those then are the main differences for me. I don't think for a moment that basically the players are any better in England, but they are far better prepared, both in coaching and training, than up in Scotland.

That competitive spirit I am talking about just has to follow when you think about it. At St Mirren we only had about 14 or 15 full-time pros whereas at Leeds

27

(*Above*) Gordon McQueen on the alert with Arsenal on the attack at Elland Road.

(*Below*) West Ham's Clyde Best contends for the ball as Gordon McQueen closes in.

the pool is much larger. In Scotland most clubs just cannot afford a large squad of players. Very few are economically sound and in my opinion only about seven of the Scottish clubs would hold their own in the English First Division: Celtic, Rangers, Hibs, Hearts, Aberdeen, and the Dundee clubs.

The rest of the Scottish First Division would be pushed to survive in the English Second Division, while the Scots Second Division boys would end up in the English Fourth Division and even non-league football.

As it is they have to sell to survive. They only get meagre crowds most of the time and that means economic problems all along the way.

That I suppose is another difference when you think about it. When I was with St Mirren our crowd would average around the 4,000 mark. Only when we played Rangers or Celtic would we top the 15,000–20,000 figure. I had played in front of a few large crowds in my Scottish league days, but when I moved to Elland Road I had to adjust to playing in front of 50,000 plus crowds each and every week.

Personally I never let it bother me. I rather enjoy it in a way. The large crowds give the game more atmosphere, flavour, importance – call it what you will.

I suppose the bigger gates mean greater pressure and that, in turn, makes for little room for mistakes. At Leeds, for instance, you are encouraged to play to your capabilities and no more. In Scotland there was greater freedom to do what you thought, but then errors were never punished to such a degree as in First Division circles.

When I look at Scottish soccer, I must be honest and admit that I doubt very much whether Celtic's monopoly of the championship is the best thing for soccer North of the border. Nine titles all in a row for Celtic is great for them but in the long run it must be slowly and surely killing off Scottish football. In England it's a different story. To win the title once is good going, never mind nine times in a row.

I'm still only 22 and as I move into my third season an established Leeds player I hope I can help the club to win the European Cup and then move on to take the World Club Championship. That would be marvellous and set up a unique first for Leeds. As one of the junior partners in the Elland Road consortium that achievement would really be something and oh, such a long, long way from my days in the Scottish Second Division!

# MATCH OF
# THE DAY

John Motson says it's not as easy
as it looks on B.B.C.

It was a cold, grey afternoon on Tyneside, with an icy rain falling and the St James's Park floodlights piercing the gloom. Frank Clark ran down the Newcastle left and crossed to the far post. Up went the blond head of John Tudor, and the ball flashed past Gary Pierce into the Wolves' net.

It was Newcastle's second goal in five minutes, it had undoubtedly clinched the two points, the home fans were delighted. But the only trouble was, Tudor was not the scorer. Just behind his right shoulder, another fair-haired Newcastle player had jumped at the same time. It was not until the players were running back to the centre that I was able to establish that Pat Howard, the centre-half, was the man who made contact.

That was just one of many moments when this particular commentator has had his heart in his mouth. Fortunately, some sort of sixth sense had prevented me from naming the wrong scorer, and I was even more relieved when my *Match of the Day* colleague, Barry Davies, admitted a few days later that he had suffered a similar experience at Newcastle only the season before.

The incident illustrates just one of the hazards of the commentator's job. Although you normally find him perched high above the action, the commentary position at St James's Park is lower than most, and it is more difficult to spot what is happening on the far side of a crowded penalty-area! How some managers get a good view of the game from the touchline bench I'll never know!

Making sure you identify players correctly is, of course, among the commentator's priorities. I don't know about the others, but I always have a few blind spots. Despite seeing them on and off the field on countless occasions, I still find myself double checking to distinguish between two Stoke players, Denis Smith and Jimmy Greenhoff. Fortunately, they play in different positions, but when Smith popped up in the attack at Leeds to head an equalizer last season, I was taken very much by surprise!

People often ask me what commentators do the rest of the week. Well, most of us work on other programmes as well, covering interviews and stories for Grandstand's *Football Preview*, for example. But you will often find one of us sitting in the Press Box or in the stand at a midweek match. Frequently, you would be right in guessing that one or both of the teams involved are shortly scheduled to appear on television, and the commentator is doing his homework on the individual players, the team formation, and any other features he can add to his background material.

I find this sort of homework invaluable. If it is at all possible to see a team play in the week or two before I cover them, then I make every effort to do so. If there is no midweek match, I will try to get the manager's permission to watch a training session.

31

John Motson went from B.B.C. radio to B.B.C. television. He says that television is 'one thousand times harder'.

Talking of managers, every commentator has his own way of preparing, but I also make a habit of talking to the manager or coach of both sides in the few days preceding the game. Obviously the nature of the job means I am covering a different team most weeks, so it is helpful to know the recent history of how each team has been playing, what the manager feels their problems have been, and so on.

The other part of my preparation involves just me and my record books. From the beginning of the season, I keep a hard-backed book in which I record the results, appearances, goalscorers, and attendances of all First and Second Division teams. Thus, if I am covering Southampton for the first time that season, I can see at a glance how many goals Mike Channon has scored, how many appearances

Terry Paine has made, and how many times Gerry O'Brien has come on as substitute.

I also record transfers, changes of manager, disciplinary proceedings, international teams, and results of European games. In addition, I have my own card index for every player in the first two Divisions, giving biographical notes such as when he joined his club, where he made his debut, and how many caps he has won for his country.

It is difficult to assess just how many hours are spent preparing for a game, but if you added together the time the process just outlined takes, and took an average throughout the season, I suppose you could truthfully say I spend two full days a week preparing for a match. Add to this the fact that I am often travelling north on a Friday, and you will gather that from Wednesday onwards I am preparing for that 90 minutes on a Saturday!

And it *is* 90 minutes, by the way! Some people still ask me whether we go back to the studio and put our commentary on the edited highlights after the match. I am afraid not! We talk over the 90 minutes and then live or die by what we have said. Once the match is over, how well it is presented on your screen that night is down to the skill and expertise of our video-tape editing team – and that, believe me, can be a far harder job than commentating!

The longer I do the job, the more difficult it becomes to say what makes a good or bad commentator. I think you, the viewers and the real fans, are the best judges of that. I suppose the chief complaint levelled against commentators over the years has been that they talk too much, and I know this was a fault I had when I first came into television. For two years, I had been doing radio commentaries on a Saturday afternoon. The task of the sound commentator is entirely different. The listener has no picture, so providing he keeps up with the play, the commentator is free to talk, describe, and enlarge to his heart's content.

When I moved to *Match of the Day*, I had a rude awakening. Suddenly, the players and the ground were there for all to see. Unless I could add anything useful to the picture, I was advised to 'shut up'! Believe me, the techniques of radio and television commentary are entirely different. Maybe it's because I was in radio first, but I would honestly say that television is one thousand times harder.

Without getting too technical, another difference in television is that the commentator can hear the producer directing his cameras through the headphones, and from time to time will receive instructions himself. Thus it requires a split concentration, 99 per cent watching what is going on in the game, but keeping half an ear open for direction or guidance from the producer.

I am often asked how much I watch the game and how much attention I pay to the monitor sets on which I see the picture that you, the viewer, are getting. My formula is simple. While the ball is in play, I watch the field, because if something happens out of the picture (i.e. an incident off the ball or a player making a run on the far side) then the viewer wants to know from the commentator! But when the ball goes out of play, the chances are the producer will cut to an appropriate close-up, and then I have to turn my eye to the monitor to make sure I am talking about the right player!

What else is the commentator there for? Again, it's a personal view, but I think without getting what the professionals would call over-tactical, he assists the viewer with the occasional pertinent remark about the run of play. Although the edited highlights usually reflect the ebb and flow of the game with uncanny accuracy, I believe we need to be aware that the viewer is only going to see, say, one third or less of the match. Thus, as the teams leave the field at the end or at half time, I always try to summarize the way the game went in that half.

The main stumbling block I have found, is that thin line between the area of reporting (and I still consider myself a journalist) and the area of tactical analysis which belongs to the professional. There is a happy medium, but it is one we are continually trying to find week after week.

Like any other football reporter, the commentator finds himself in regular contact with managers and players in the game. I have always found them readily co-operative if there is anything I want to know, and last summer I learned a lot from listening to the professionals talking at one of the F.A.'s coaching courses at Lilleshall.

Finally, I really feel I ought to underline that although the commentator has the glamorous job, a football programme such as *Match of the Day* is a real team effort. On any Saturday, over 100 people are involved in some way, from Editor Sam Leitch through to the riggers who actually put the equipment on those high commentary rostrums.

The two teams on the field are fighting against each other. Our team is often fighting against time, fading light, technical hitches and a hundred and one minor problems. So, every week, we are trying to win our *Match of the Day. Thank you for your support!*

On the commentary position at Roker Park, Sunderland, John Motson during a typical day's work.

TOMMY HUTCHISON (COVENTRY CITY)

MALCOLM MACDONALD (NEWCASTLE UNITED)

JOHN CONNOLLY (EVERTON)

MICK JONES (LEEDS UNITED)

# VILLA CAN REIGN AGAIN

## says Dennis Shaw
### Chief Soccer Writer of
### the Birmingham Evening Mail

In pre-war days there was a rather well-worn phrase that Birmingham was famous for three reasons: politician Joe Chamberlain, the Bull Ring . . . and Aston Villa. Sadly, in more recent years, there has been a cynical tendency to compare the club more readily with the Hall of Memory.

Can Aston Villa be great again? Or is the majestic Villa Park stadium to remain a monument to the past resurrected into the limelight only for F.A. Cup semi-finals and representative matches? The red-brick façade oozes tradition. The very atmosphere of the ground breathes a sense of history despite having been given a face-lift here and there to bring it into the 20th century.

What Villa desperately needs is a well-equipped stadium in line with the needs of the 1970s while retaining its links with a glorious past. It is on the pitch where the problems lie and where the key to the famous club's future can be turned.

Now would indeed be an appropriate time for the re-building which has been going on for five years or more to gain the momentum needed to lift the club back into the First Division, Europe, and a future to match the past. Last year was Aston Villa's Centenary year and it began unhappily in the Second Division rather than, more fittingly, in the First Division.

It has been one of the saddest features of soccer in recent times that the decline of Aston Villa has coincided with similar falls experienced by Preston and Blackburn, other clubs who were giants of the early days of football.

The reason is not hard to trace and is more than coincidence. In their glory years, admittedly going back to the start of the century, these clubs were established as the forerunners. It seemed they had only to go on in their normal way to stay on top. But other clubs had to strive to build themselves up to compare with them. Eventually the order changed. It was a case of ambition versus complacency and

40

Those who got away: Gerry Hitchens, Derek Dougan, and Danny Blanchflower.

ambition won. The Villa, Preston, and Blackburn, lived with tradition for too long and, apart from the odd year or two, have been paying the price ever since.

But compared to Preston and Blackburn, Villa have one enormous advantage. They are a big city club. They have sprawling suburbia all around them, new housing estates, new motorway links, new industries.

What is more, with the building of the National Exhibitions centre near Birmingham, the Midlands will become more than ever an international trade centre and so the scope is limitless. There are, perhaps, clubs in the world with more potential than Aston Villa, but not many.

Having said that it must also be pointed out that achievement has not matched that potential for more than 50 years. Villa last won the First Division title in 1910. Since then they have won the F.A. Cup twice, the Football League Cup once, in its first year, and have been relegated to the Second Division on three occasions and to the Third Division once.

Why the failure? Again the answer is not too difficult to find. The clubs who have had spells of consistent success since the war – Wolves, Manchester United, Spurs, Leeds, Everton, Liverpool, Arsenal, Manchester City, and the rest – have done so because of either a shrewd buying policy or a productive youth development scheme or both.

On both these fronts Villa's record has similarly been sadly lacking. The only local player Villa have steered to full England level in the last 30 years was Eddie

41

The newcomers: Ian Ross, Chris Nicholl, and Ray Graydon.

Lowe, from nearby Halesowen. That was in 1946!

Another factor is that over the same period many stars have been sold to continue fine careers elsewhere: Lowe to Fulham, Danny Blanchflower to Spurs, Tommy Thompson to Preston, Gerry Hitchens to Inter-Milan, Harry Burrows to Stoke, Derek Dougan to Peterborough. More than 10 years ago Villa almost made it on the youth front with the famous Mercer Minors, nurtured by Joe Mercer. There were Alan Deakin, Mike Tindall, John Sleeuwenhoek, Harry Burrows, and Charlie Aitken. But they climbed no higher than sixth in the First Division and the club has been sliding ever since until recently.

So much for history. But just where do Villa stand now? Happily, since a public issue of shares six years ago and a reconstructed board of directors, there has been a steady, if not spectacular, improvement.

Initially under the management of Tommy Docherty crowds, which had fallen to the 11,000 mark, swarmed back, new players were bought, and the slow climb was under way.

Docherty was replaced by Vic Crowe as the progress slowly simmered down. Villa went from the Second Division to the Third Division and back and in successive seasons led the promotion race only to fall away disappointingly.

But in this time some selective buying has taken place – defenders Ian Ross (Liverpool), Chris Nicholl (Luton), John Robson (Derby), and goalkeeper Jim Cumbes (West Bromwich Albion); and winger Ray Graydon (Bristol Rovers) gave Villa the nucleus of a First Division-class staff.

42

In addition Crowe picked up on a free transfer from Liverpool the young full-back, John Gidman, who featured in a Villa team of youngsters who won the F.A. Youth Cup. Gidman then progressed into the first team to become a player who will attract the attention of England along with striker Brian Little.

Through it all, for the past 12 years, has survived just one player, namely full-back Charlie Aitken who in season 1973–74 beat the legendary Billy Walker's League appearance record for the club of 478.

An analysis at the end of 1973–74 revealed that although Villa had faded in mid-season, they were at last putting together a combined policy of shrewd buying and youth development. Unfortunately from Manager Crowe's viewpoint the available cash ran out and the shortage of a consistently successful striker to replace Andy Lochhead held them back. It became necessary to balance the books by selling in order to buy or by making player-exchange deals. Sheer economics made progress slow down.

One contradictory situation at Villa Park has been that their greatest strength – their enormous following – can be their greatest weakness. Supporters, disenchanted by more than 60 years without the First Division title and more than 15 years without the F.A. Cup, want success more quickly than it has been coming. And sharpening the appetite of Villa fans for success has been the fact that nearby Birmingham City made it into the First Division before them. The fact that City

The youngsters: John Gidman and Brian Little.

found life in the First Division to consist largely of fighting relegation did not ease the pain for Villa.

Blues, in fact, had struck pure gold in actually finding a one-hundred-per-cent Brummie lad in Bob Latchford, who could not only score goals but who wore the white shirt of England along with Trevor Francis at Under-23 level.

Villa fans will only be happy when Villa are one of the country's top clubs, winning honours, performing in Europe, finding top-class youngsters (preferably from Brum) and supplying them to England. The odd six-figure signing would be the icing on a very palatable cake. Can it happen? Current indications are that it might. For the sake of contentment in hundreds of thousands of West Midlands homes, it must.

The man who broke Billy Walker's Villa League appearance record, Charlie Aitken.

# CAPTAINS OF ENGLAND

## by Kenneth Wheeler

England's team lined up in front of the Royal Box at Wembley with the Welsh facing them. It was January 27, 1943, so the predominant attire among the 75,000 spectators was battledress. The occasion marked, for all concerned, a brief but glamorous escape from the realities of war.

Pausing before the sturdy R.A.F. officer who stood at the head of the line, the F.A. Chairman, Mr Brook Hirst, told King George VI: 'Sir, this is Eddie Hapgood, the England captain.'

The King asked Hapgood: 'How many times have you played for England?'

'Forty-three,' was the proud reply. This total may not sound remarkable today: and, even then, twelve of Hapgood's appearances had been in unofficial wartime games like this one. But everyone present was prepared to accept 43 as the new record, superseding Bob Crompton's collection of 42 caps before the First World War.

'And how old are you?'

'Thirty-four, sir.'

The King smiled. 'The same figures reversed,' he observed. His Majesty was later reminded, this was also the 34th occasion on which Hapgood had captained England, another record.

In 100 years of vast change, 60 different men have captained England. From Cuthbert Ottaway, the brilliant dribbling star of the first international match ever played (Scotland v England in 1872), there followed a long succession of famous Corinthian characters, appointed mostly on a match-to-match basis. Then the solidly-built Bob Crompton of the wax-tipped moustache, the first professional to captain England over a lengthy spell, and finally to Bobby Moore, the last established skipper. But Edris Albert Hapgood, left-back of the Arsenal F.C., must be considered the first truly great England captain, first of that great trinity of Hapgood, Wright, and Moore which spans 250 caps and 30 active years.

Eddie Hapgood was a natural leader and a defender of world class.

George Hardwick of Middlesbrough, the man who preceded Billy Wright as England captain.

Like Wright and Moore, Hapgood was a natural leader but a self-made defender of world class. A former Bristol milkman, he weighed a mere 9 stone 6 pounds at the start of his Arsenal career, the lightest back in the League. He suffered from a soft skull and, in fact, frequently knocked himself out in the act of heading a ball heavy with mud. But Hapgood was a man of tremendous courage, and he trained himself to be iron hard. At the same time he developed his ball control, his kicking, and his keen positional sense, until he was recognized as the best left-back in the business.

After serving under Roy Goodall and Tom Cooper, Hapgood was made England captain on November 14, 1934, when six of his Arsenal colleagues were also picked in the team to meet Italy. This game was only 15 minutes old when an Italian elbow smashed into the new England captain's face to break his nose. But Hapgood, who knew no fear, soon returned with his nose in plaster to lead England to victory in the notoriously brutal game which history remembers as 'the Battle of Highbury'.

Hapgood went on to lead England for nine years on every occasion he played, except one, against Finland at Helsinki, when George Male, his Arsenal full-back partner, was captain. Under Hapgood, England were exposed for the first time to a stiff and determined challenge by other European countries. But his team had no manager, and no special preparation for its tasks. Tactics were usually decided by last-minute discussion in the dressing room.

Increasing political tension during the late 'thirties made Hapgood's role

46

Billy Wright, seen exchanging pennants with Italian captain Armando Segato, played 90 matches as captain over a period of 11 years.

additionally onerous, but he took politics in his stride and revealed surprisingly mature qualities as a diplomat. For an £8 match fee this country was served by a supreme footballer, captain, manager, and ambassador rolled into one!

Perhaps his most spectacular triumph was leading England to a 6–3 victory over Germany at the Berlin Olympic Stadium in 1938 before Adolf Hitler and 110,000 heiling Nazis. But in victory or defeat, Hapgood never lost his dignity, nor allowed any team-mate to do so.

Hapgood himself always named his greatest match as England's 2–1 win over Scotland in 1939, their first at Hampden for 12 years. In those days the annual

Johnny Haynes chaired by England players Peter Swan, Jim Armfield, and Mike McNeil in 1961. Haynes had received the British International Championship Trophy after England's 9–3 defeat of Scotland.

encounter of football's oldest enemies was still the one that mattered most to both sets of players, and this time Hapgood excelled in both his encouragement of others and by his personal example.

But after the war priorities changed, and England's entry into global competition necessitated the appointment of a team manager and a different sort of captain. Different, yes, but in no sense inferior, because though the captain's tactical responsibility was now lessened he now had another – the need to develop an affinity with his manager and learn to think along parallel lines.

Walter Winterbottom, the new England manager, admits that he did not immediately recognize Billy Wright's suitability for this testing role. This was not surprising, for the enthusiastic young Wolverhampton wing-half was a mere beginner compared with such experienced colleagues as Swift, Franklin, Lawton, Carter, and Matthews. But after an unpromising beginning, when his club wondered whether he could ever acquire the muscle and inches necessary to make the grade, Billy had worked with unflagging determination to achieve full stature in every sense. Then, in 1948, when the need arose to find a successor to George Hardwick of Middlesborough, Billy was elected England captain because of his dependability, and his sustained and reliable level of performance.

He grew into the job like a hero from the pages of fiction. He was fair haired, blue eyed, clean living, honest, and friendly. He proved unfailingly sympathetic and helpful to other players, always a model of good sportsmanship. Such was his fame and influence that he survived England's shattering defeat at the hands of the U.S.A. in the 1950 World Cup, and also the team's annihiliation by Hungary at Wembley in 1953, and continued to lead until his retirement in 1959 when his highly successful, overall record was beyond criticism. Wright played 105 matches for England, each one under the management of Walter Winterbottom, 90 of them as captain over a period of 11 years.

First Ronnie Clayton, then Johnny Haynes, took over from Wright. Haynes seemed set for a long and successful run, but a car accident in Blackpool in 1962 cost him his England place and he was succeeded by Jim Armfield. Then, during England's first tour under Alf Ramsey's management in 1963, Armfield was injured, and in Bratislava the 22-year-old East Londoner, Bobby Moore, became the youngest ever to be appointed England captain.

Alf Ramsey, who had himself captained England on rare occasions when Billy Wright had been missing, told young Moore: 'Whatever you do on the field, whatever decisions you think are necessary, you'll have my full backing.' He proved as good as his word, while Moore found a job which at once fitted him like a glove. 'I like being captain,' he said, 'I enjoy the responsibility.'

49

Bobby Moore led England to World Cup success in 1966 and made a record 108 England appearances.

Like his famous predecessors, Moore had to work harder than most at the start to make up for lack of natural brilliance. And, partly as a result, he developed rare ability to read a game. He was to complete a record 108 appearances for England, including leading his side to World Cup victory in 1966 and was deservedly chosen as the outstanding Man of the Tournament.

With the loss of pace and quick reaction that gradually affects sportsmen over 30, Moore inevitably began to fade towards the end of 1973 and could no longer be regarded as the automatic choice he had been for so long. Emlyn Hughes, the enthusiastic Liverpool player, was chosen as captain when Don Revie assumed control in 1974.

Moore never had quite the same responsibility to carry as Eddie Hapgood, nor did he completely fit the image of a second Billy Wright, but like them he was the perfect leader for his time. Despite much greater pressures, and the much higher standard of play demanded of him and his team, Bobby has still emerged with a character comparable with the Corinthian tradition, while in partnership with Sir Alf Ramsey the success achieved in real terms was incomparable.

50

# MIRACLES TAKE A LITTLE LONGER

## Pat Gregory

Hon. Secretary of the Women's Football Association,
tells how women's football became established

'Girls aren't meant to play football,' snorted my Victorian father. But a few weeks later he was turning out, albeit reluctant and shivering, to cheer on his two daughters in the first match of their newly-formed team.

That sums up the attitude of most men, parents or boy friends, to what they would call the hilarious spectacle of women's football. But in only six years, those that had come to scoff had to admit that we girl footballers had something, even if only a more alluring shape in shorts and shirts.

Women's football isn't new to Britain; indeed, few people realize that it has been played here since the early years of this century, although in 1921 the football authorities branded it as unsuitable for the gentler sex.

Our playing struggles have been matched off the field by unceasing efforts to bring the nation to realize that women's football is a viable sport. For many years Dick Kerr's ladies' team from Preston raised a great deal of money for charity and in 1949 the Manchester Corinthians team was formed. Indeed, it became a founder member of the Women's Football Association.

When in June 1967 I started my own club with a nucleus of equally-keen school

England's first women's international team seen at Wembley before the match against Scotland in November 1972. Fourth from right, back row, is Sheila Parker the captain.

friends in North London, our only opposition was from boys' teams. An advertisement in a national soccer magazine produced replies from boys' clubs willing to provide competition.

Fortunately, it also brought a letter from Arthur Hobbs, a carpenter from Deal, Kent, who was later to become the first Secretary of the Women's F.A. He was then organizing his second ladies' football tournament and invited my team to join in. We quickly learned that the few other women's teams then in existence knew far more about football than we did.

But from the contacts made at the tournament came the beginning of a small League of teams from the London and Bedfordshire areas. An invitation to tour Czechoslovakia followed, and the League's Representative Team became possibly the first Western women's football team to play behind the Iron Curtain. It was a highly successful return visit after the tour made earlier by our Czech hosts.

Though the international bond went little noticed except in our immediate local circle, women's football was beginning to crack the seemingly impervious surface of official indifference. Our regular League programme helped persuade the local council to permit the use of a park pitch.

At the beginning of 1969 the Central Council of Physical Recreation became aware of the growing interest among girls in playing football. Its officers encouraged Arthur Hobbs to consider the formation of a governing body and in a few short months the W.F.A. became a properly constituted body with 38 founder member clubs.

Heady stuff, but champagne was to follow – a Christmas present in the shape of the abolition by the all-male Football Association Council of the 1921 Law

Midfield player Margaret 'Paddy' McGroarty with England manager Tommy Tranter, a senior F.A. coach.

which had forbidden women to play football.

Now we were on our way. All the hard work, all the scoffing – from men and women alike – was forgotten. By the W.F.A.'s first birthday the new Association became eligible for membership of the C.C.P.R. and the constant battle for funds was slightly but thankfully eased with an administrative grant from that body.

The W.F.A. Mitre Challenge Trophy was our first taste of sponsorship. We cannot hope to compete with the glamour of the F.A. Cup but our trophy competition is having its own modest success. In the first three years of the W.F.A. Mitre Trophy, Scotland and England have provided the finalists. Although the English club, Southampton, have won each final it was a triumph for women's football. The Scots, living up to the reputation their male counterparts have won in world football, went down fighting and with honour.

1972 saw the creation of the first England team. With the steady growth of the sport in every Continent, a European or World Cup competition cannot be far off, and the girls of the U.K.'s national teams will be equal to the challenge.

I would not like to leave you with the impression that women footballers are a branch of the 'burn the bra' brigade, although I have no doubt there are fervent women's lib supporters playing football somewhere in the world, and, I believe, playing it well. Although the battle of the sexes must play some part, as it always will, I am sure that woman's three most widely-exploited attributes, charm, tact, and patience, must inevitably help us to win, even though as the saying goes 'miracles take a little longer'.

We have plenty of enthusiasts willing to work miracles and provide the courage and faith as exemplified by one of our earliest players – Ginny Howard, who broke her back in a road accident. Although her footballing days were ended, Ginny fought back and entered several events in the Paraplegic Olympic Games.

And for faith, I have to admire the keen eleven-year-old schoolgirl who, touchingly I think, wrote to me time after time asking how she could play for England. I hope I encouraged her and I am pleased to report that she is now a member of a ladies' club. I shall watch her progress with interest.

Action during the 1974 England *v* Wales match which England won 5–1.

# THE GREATS
# OF ENGLISH
# FOOTBALL

## by Sir Alf Ramsey

During my life in football as a player and a manager I have met and got to know many footballers, and many of them can be classed as great. Others have approached greatness.

If I think of English players alone, names come flooding back; men who by their individual skill or brilliant team performance were a delight to see in action. I had better refrain from mentioning any by name as I obviously would not wish to offend by omitting a name, however unwittingly. But perhaps I would be forgiven if I merely mentioned the Spurs team with which I was usually associated as a player: Ditchburn, Ramsay, Willis, Nicholson, Clarke, Burgess, Duquemin, Bennett, Bailey, Medley, and Walters.

I am not for one moment suggesting that we were a great team, but I am sure you will agree that there were several players in that team who, as public entertainers, were experts at the job.

I have, therefore, decided to play safe and have selected as my 'great' players men who I think most will agree have a very special place in the history of English football during the past 20 or 30 years.

They are Gordon Banks, Bobby Charlton, Tom Finney, Jimmy Greaves, Johnny Haynes, Stanley Matthews, Bobby Moore, and Billy Wright.

### Gordon Banks

As I indicated in my message in his testimonial match programme, Gordon represents for me all that is good in football. His enforced retirement as a result

A post-retirement picture of Gordon Banks on his way abroad to make some personal appearances in the Far East.

of a car crash was a severe blow to British football. Between the goal-posts, he was unsurpassed; he made everything look so easy and yet, when the occasion demanded, his reflexes were such that he would frequently reach the 'impossible' shot or header. I believe that he was the best goalkeeper in the world during his peak years. His dedication to the game, his masterly skill, and his loyalty are qualities which cannot be over-praised. He played 73 times for England and during his League career was with Chesterfield, Leicester City, and Stoke City.

*Bobby Charlton*

What can I say about Bobby that has not already been said or written? He was surely every boy's football hero, producing, as he did, the devastating shot which won so many matches. But Bobby was more than a great kicker of the ball. In midfield or as an attacking player he was a great tactician. His anticipation and ability to size up a situation in a split-second have often won him possession of the ball at vital moments in the game. His defence-splitting passes have created untold goal-scoring chances for his colleagues. Off the field, he was always the unassuming personality he was when playing. He was a tremendous worker and treated every training session conscientiously no matter what the match ahead. In his 106 matches for England he scored 49 goals. He was a Manchester United player throughout his playing career from 1954 to 1973.

Bobby Charlton seen with his brother Jackie in 1965. Both were to play in England's legendary World Cup team in 1966.

Exuberant horseplay during World Cup training in 1958. Tom Finney and Bobby Charlton give Billy Wright a lift.

Finney and Wright limbering up. Between them they accumulated 181 England caps.

## Tom Finney

Mention Stanley Matthews and you almost invariably think of at the same time his contemporary, Tom Finney, a classical footballer if ever there was one. By a very deceptive run and by his skill at making a defender move the wrong way in the tackle, Tom was able to glide through and find himself in a position to shoot at goal or slide the ball backwards to an on-coming colleague. Once in possession, he was most difficult to dispossess. Everything he did was dainty, precise, and unruffled. Unlike Matthews, he was a frequent goalscorer, able to shoot accurately along the carpet with either foot. Indeed he could play equally well at outside-right or outside-left. He graced our football fields from 1946 to 1960 and played for Preston North End throughout that time. He made 76 appearances for England.

## Jimmy Greaves

Jimmy was probably the slickest goalscorer in the game in the post-war years. He showed by sheer opportunism and alertness how half-chances could be turned into goals. Deadly accurate inside the 18-yard area, he would tackle strongly to gain possession and once the ball was in shooting range, he would give the goalkeeper little chance. With his exhilarating forward play, Jimmy was a great favourite with London crowds, first with Chelsea, then Tottenham Hotspur. I think he might have been an even greater player if he had not felt unsettled at various times during his career. He had great flair and his quick brain and speed off the mark made him a most dangerous forward to hold.

Jimmy Greaves, man of flair and speed.

Idol of the soccer fans in the early sixties was Johnny Haynes.

*Johnny Haynes*
Many will proclaim that Johnny Haynes epitomizes the perfect footballer. Most
certainly, his skill, judgment, tactical appreciation, and control, had few equals.
He was always able to imprint upon a game his authority and could influence
play by 'taking things by the scruff of the neck' and switching defence to attack.
His ball-control and passing were superb and he frequently demoralized defences
by tailor-made passes which found their target. Johnny was also a capable captain,
using his natural footballing ability and know-all to full advantage. He played all
his football for Fulham and won 56 caps.

59

*Sir Stanley Matthews*

If you are one of the fortunate people to have seen Stanley Matthews in action, you will never forget his dazzling football as long as you live. What an outstanding example of physical fitness the man was – remember he first represented Stoke City in his teens and played his last League match after his 50th birthday. It has been said that he would not have succeeded against the tight defences of the 'seventies, but I believe that Stanley would have mesmerized his opponents just as effectively as he did 20–30 years ago. With the ball at his feet, he could dance his way past defender after defender with only inches to spare and would appear to be virtually impossible to dispossess. The crowds flocked to see him wherever he played. His brand of individual artistry is rare among present-day footballers.

Stanley Matthews is presented to the Duke of Edinburgh before the 1953 F.A. Cup-Final.

Sir Alf Ramsey's soccer partnership with Bobby Moore spanned the 1966 World Cup and a host of other international successes.

## Bobby Moore

No review of this kind would be complete without a reference to Bobby Moore, who continues to entertain us playing for Fulham where he transferred from West Ham. Bobby played for England since 1962 and has never given a poor performance. He has now reached a total of 108 international appearances, a record which will be difficult to better. Strong, dependable, determined, and a real professional, Bobby will surely be remembered for all time as one of the greats, the man who led England to success in the 1966 World Cup.

## Billy Wright

The first international player to reach 100 caps, Billy was one of the most dedicated players I have ever known. Originally a right half-back, Billy assumed the centre-half role in a masterly fashion and quickly developed into a defender of great tenacity and skill. Very powerful and fit, Billy was particularly agile and, in spite of comparatively small stature, was able to meet on equal terms the tallest centre-forwards which he faced. He was an excellent header of the ball. For many seasons Billy was England's captain and perhaps I can best describe the way he led his team by saying that he inspired by example rather than by generalship. His determination, his drive, and his 100 per cent effort was there for all to see.

Billy Wright acknowledges the applause of the crowd at Wembley before his 100th international in 1959.

# SOCCER MAN AND BOY

## Jackie Charlton

Middlesbrough manager, and former England player, talks
about the things which have changed and those which have not.

I came into football as a 15-year-old kid. I am still in football at 38 as a manager of a First Division club. In that time I have seen sweeping changes in the attitude to training and to training methods. What has not changed, of course, is that a player still needs application to win his place in the team and tenacity to stay there.

In those early days, we were required to do a tremendous amount of lappng and a lot of five-a-sides. But there was little emphasis on tactics, systems of play, and other aspects of a footballer's preparation which are taken for granted today.

The demands made on top-class players and the stresses imposed on them are terrific. They are required to possess a standard of fitness that would almost qualify them as all-round athletes. Coupled with this outstanding physical specification they must also have the capacity to take knocks, recover from difficult situations in a condition of near-exhaustion, and then respond to new situations calling for redoubled effort.

Fitness training today doesn't usually take as long as it used to. The work is packed into shorter sessions of very intense activity, almost always without the ball. Ball practices are carried out once we have got the hard work out of the way. This allows us to concentrate on quality.

Because we are training players virtually seven days a week a lot of thought goes into devising variations on the same type of training. We must keep players interested in what they are doing and see that they enjoy the training. This is the only way to maintain the level of motivation necessary in top-class football.

Almost all our ball practices are carried out in various opposed situations because we believe that if you have to perform under pressure on Saturday afternoon you may as well learn to perform under pressure during the week. We also spend time explaining to players the reasons behind the routines they carry out.

Players have to maintain a high level of fitness throughout the year. No longer do they get a complete lay-off as used to be the case in the past. We feel that to go

Jackie Charlton greets the crowd at his testimonial match at Elland Road, Leeds, on the night he was confirmed as Middlesbrough's new manager.

out of training completely and then try to re-capture it takes far too much time, so we prefer players, even during their holidays, to keep up some sort of basic fitness training.

My old club, Leeds United, always put the well-being of their players before anything else. Great pains are taken over general health and the treatment of injuries is never neglected.

Here at Middlesbrough, as at Leeds, we try to make the lads feel important, to give them a sense of responsibility, not only to the club but also to the town they represent. As a player I was constantly reminded that my behaviour away from home, whether in England or abroad, with Leeds or with England, was important to myself, my club, my country, and to football itself.

English League football is the hardest competition of its kind in the world. Now in addition to this very tough assignment, clubs are invading the European scene more and more. Consider the case of Leeds United. At one time they were involved in the F.A. Cup semi-final, European Cup semi-final, and the League Championship in the same hectic week. They were committed to about 70 matches per season.

The pressure of big match commitments on top clubs shows no signs of letting up. Obviously you can't make it at that level of output without hard and un-relenting effort. But because you enjoy the game it's not so arduous or so dull having to get through all that fitness training. Of course, the financial rewards are there, too, enough to take care of you for the rest of your life. You can't all win, but you can all enjoy having a go.

Jackie on the ITV World Cup panel with Derek Dougan, Brian Clough, and Malcolm Allison

Jackie Charlton takes an armful of Middlesbrough tracksuits in his stride.

# THE 'MYTH' OF SCOTTISH SOCCER GENIUS

There is a measure of truth in it,
writes Bill Brown, London Sports
Editor of the Glasgow *Evening Times*

The Glasgow police pipe band in action at the World Cup Opening Ceremony at Frankfurt Waldstadium.

Alex James (*above*) and Hughie Gallacher (*right*), two of the immortals of Scottish football admired and imitated by schoolchildren over the years.

Are Scotland the nation of natural footballers folklore would have us believe? Is every other lad there a likely Willie Morgan, Denis Law, or Billy Bremner? Not quite. They are no better, in the main, at imposing their will upon the ball than are their counterparts in England or in almost any other country where the sphere is chased around.

How then has the myth come about of a special Scottish aptitude for the soccer arts? And why do the English and others subscribe to it in spite of evidence that for many years most Scottish clubs have been playing football the hard and fast English way? And that until recently it has been the devil's own job to get a Scottish international team to work together as a unit in two successive matches?

Like most myths there is a measure of truth in the story. The truth of this particular matter is that a climate has been created in Scotland this century which fosters football practically as a way of life, in much the same fashion as the Welsh dote on Rugby Union, and the Americans subscribe to baseball and their own killing brand of football.

Scotsmen have been conditioned by their environment and their elders to feel that supremacy at football is one of the noblest achievements of man. The home-based Scottish football star is an object of veneration such as is scarcely known south of the Border. And there are the Anglos to help embellish the legend of a nation with natural-born football gifts.

Forty or fifty years ago when the Scottish flair for the game was seen to be at its height, the Glasgow area – and indeed much of the Lowlands of Scotland – seemed to be full of football pitches. They offered a cheap form of exercise, leisure, and entertainment in a depressed industrial society. There were Corporation fields, makeshift pitches. On any flattish piece of waste ground or tenement back-court at any time of the day, spindly schoolchildren and members of the army of young unemployed, believing themselves to be budding Alex James's and Hughie Gallachers and Alan Mortons, would be chasing balls of various sizes.

This point has to be made: most of the football that was played in that far-off heyday of the Scottish game was of the kick-and-rush variety. Seldom would the discerning eye note in a week's watching more than a couple of youngsters with natural sway or the ability to time the dribble so that the opponent was lost.

But the Scots are a persevering breed, as well as being great self-trumpeters.

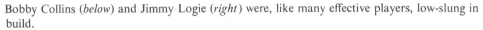

Bobby Collins (*below*) and Jimmy Logie (*right*) were, like many effective players, low-slung in build.

And with such a concentration on the one sport to the exclusion of most other forms of athletic activity except golf (where, incidentally, the same argument holds good), and with plenty of professional League teams to aspire to, there were bound to be many lads who would, through sheer application, develop into skilled ball manipulators. Thus, the legend that had been fostered earlier in the century gained substance.

Even when it was palpably obvious that the Scots were no longer cocks of the walk the story persisted. What the 'Wembley Wizards' did to the English is looked upon and spoken of as something in the nature of a visit by super-intellectual Martians. If you look at the other side of the coin, and see what the English and other nations have done to the Scots in their poorer years, much less is made of it by the conquerors than by the Scots themselves who look upon such defeats as akin to a national disaster. It is this intense national commitment that both breeds and nourishes legend.

Curiously the English, not the Scots, were the first dribblers of the game. And the Scots actually started off the legend of their 'natural-born' gifts not by dribbling but by passing the ball to one another. They were in fact the originators of soccer

as a truly team game, and it was this understanding of how effective passing could be that gave them the edge for years over English teams.

Having tried to dispel some of the mist clinging to the Scottish football scene, I shall now do a smart about-face, and suggest that although Scotsmen in general may not be natural-born footballers, they have certain inbuilt features, physical and temperamental, that enable them to respond to the challenge of the game.

Consider many of the great Scottish players down the years such as Alex James, Hughie Gallacher, Alan Morton, Bobby Collins, Jimmy Logie, Billy Bremner, Dave Mackay, John White, Willie Henderson, and there is one common factor about them: they are all low-slung. As the Scottish phrase (translated) has it: good stuff goes into small bulk.

This has given them grip on the ground, all-round balance, tenacity on the ball. They have been able to turn what, in other fields, might be a physical disadvantage into an asset by playing the ball 'along the carpet'. It is difficult to dispossess a smallish, determined man who is crouched over the ball, without actually fouling him. Two of the greatest players England ever possessed, Stanley Matthews and Tom Finney, had this particular low-slung build.

Athletically, because of their typically short, stocky frames, the Scots make fine middle- and long-distance runners. This quality of hardness and persistence, brought to football, turns them into 90-minute players of the kind that has always commended itself to Sir Alf Ramsey, among others.

Then, of course, there is the undoubted fact that Scots are weaned to believe

Billy Bremner (*below*) and Denis Law (*right*) in action in the 1974 World Cup final series. Bremner is seen beating Brazil's Roberto Rivelino in the drawn Group Two match at Frankfurt. Law is making a breakthrough in the match against Zaire at Dortmund which Scotland won 2-0.

they are destined for greatness – and what better way to prove it to England, the old enemy, than by going South and becoming a general with the big clubs? There is, therefore, a will to succeed.

With no research at all, I can bring to your attention men from North of the Border who occupy key roles in the South: Billy Bremner (Leeds), Ken Burns (Birmingham), Willie Morgan (Manchester United), Peter Cormack (Liverpool), Eddie Kelly (Arsenal), Willie Carr (Coventry), Archie Gemmill (Derby), Jim Smith (Newcastle), Bobby Kerr (Sunderland).

When one reflects that England's finest football team, Leeds United, were primed with excellent Scottish players – Bremner, Lorimer, McQueen, the two Grays, and Jordan, besides goalkeeper Harvey – it would appear that the Scots do have something special to offer.

To keep the thing in perspective, it has to be pointed out that every one of those Scottish imports has been improved no end as a player by contact with that remarkable manager, Don Revie. Ironically enough, at Elland Road it seems to be a case of the Scots admitting, 'England and Don Revie made me'.

Mind you, Revie is married to a Scotswoman.

# Who are the TOP EURO CLUBS OF THE 70s?

## asks Bob Oxby
### of the *Daily Telegraph*

The football writer who has the temerity to suggest that one particular club in Britain is the best will, even if he picks Leeds United, be inundated with letters of protest. His postbag will bulge with correspondence extolling the virtues of Liverpool, Celtic, Arsenal, and the rest. Every fan thinks his favourite team is better than all the others.

I shudder to think what would happen if the age-old dream of a European League ever became a reality. How could the authorities agree on the clubs to be allowed to join? If, for example, they decided to start the competition in 1978, who could predict which would be England's top club by then? It might be Leeds

Two of the Ajax Amsterdam stars around whose skills the club's greatness has been built. *Above:* Piet Keizer and *below* Johann Neeskens scoring from the penalty-spot against West Germany in the 1974 World Cup Final.

The legendary Ferenc Puskas of Real Madrid.

but, then, it might be anyone else. Even a team currently in the Third Division could have emerged suddenly as a Championship winning side.

On the face of it, the most obvious method of selection would be to choose the team which had won the Championship the most times. History tells us that Arsenal and Liverpool, with eight Championships apiece, should head the list. But there could be no guarantee that, by 1978, they would still be in the front rank or even in the First Division. One need only consider what has happened to Manchester United (seven titles), and Aston Villa and Sunderland (six each), to get the message.

It is this constant shift of power which makes people describe the English First Division as the most testing in the world. In most other countries, one or two clubs seem to dominate year after year. If someone were going to select the Scottish representatives, for example, they would look no further than Celtic or Rangers. In 83 years of Scottish League history up to the start of 1974, one or the other has taken the Championship all but 13 times.

In Italy, the two Northern clubs, Juventus and Internazionale, with their vast resources, continue to dominate despite the unexpected progress made by the intimidating Lazio side of Rome. Here some may feel that a reputation for rough play should be an automatic barrier to admission.

No one would dispute which the Dutch representatives should be. Ajax Amsterdam, who began 1974 with a sensational 6–0 defeat of A.C. Milan, won the European Champions' Cup for the third year running in the summer of 1973.

In recent years, Ajax have dominated Dutch and European football in a way unknown since the great Real Madrid side of the 1950s. Strangely, the international successes were a long time coming and it was not until the arrival of the supremely-gifted Johann Cruyff in 1966 that their fortunes became transformed.

The great architect of the team who built around the skills of Piet Keizer, a devastating forward, Johann Neeskens, the attacking midfield, and Barry Hulshoff, a superb centre-back, was the demanding manager-coach, Rinus Michels. The authoritarian Dutchman caused a sensation by leaving for Barcelona, for whom he subsequently signed Cruyff, straight after the first European Cup triumph in 1971. At first, Michels' departure seemed a disaster, but it became a blessing.

His successor, the little known Rumanian, Stefan Kovacs, came from Steaua Bucharest, the Army side, and, under his more fluent and liberal direction, Ajax flowered magically. Kovacs simply allowed his gifted players to express themselves, and they did so with memorable results.

Barcelona, for so long forced to play second fiddle to the virtuosity of Real Madrid, had a moderate start under Michels, but the arrival of Cruyff, who was ineligible for the first four months of his new career, enabled them to serve notice

Alfredo Di Stefano (*behind ball*) representing F.I.F.A. against England at Wembley in 1963.

that they intended to become Spain's major club. Real remain powerful despite the loss of Miguel Munoz, their manager, who had been a brilliantly creative half-back in the team which won the European Cup five years running.

That legendary team, which included Di Stefano, Gento, and Puskas, three of the greatest forwards who ever lived, set a pattern at club level which neither Real, nor anyone else for that matter, have been able to match.

Today Real, with Amancio, a great Spanish inside-forward and Pirri, the midfield player, still possess the resources to recapture their old greatness. Like Barcelona, they imported a world-class star in Gunther Netzer, the German international midfield player, but he had difficulty in settling down.

In neighbouring Portugal, Benfica, the 'Eagles of Lisbon', remain the outstanding club despite a considerable decline from the halcyon days of the early 1960s when they won the European Cup in successive years. With the seemingly immortal Eusebio still producing his magic, and brilliant young strikers such as Jordao coming through, their place in any European League would be automatic.

But the balance of soccer power at club level has shifted away from Spain and Portugal. West Germany and, to a lesser extent, East Germany, have made remarkable strides.

Helmut Schoen, the West German team manager, built a magnificent international side simply by drawing on men from two clubs, Borussia Moenchengladbach and Bayern Munich, who have dominated the Bundesliga for the past six years.

Gerd Muller, whose phenomenal goalscoring helped to make Bayern Munich one of the top Euro clubs. Muller beats Dutchman Krol to score in the World Cup Final.

Borussia, studded with outstanding players such as Berti Vogts, Josef Heynckes, and Johnny Rupp, have been able to withstand even the loss of Netzer. Bayern, calling upon the immense gifts of Franz Beckenbauer, the phenomenal goalscoring of Gerd Muller, and the glowing promise of Paul Breitner, have suggested that they could become one of the best club sides of the decade.

The regularity with which European clubs meet in the three Cup competitions has enabled the overall level to rise over the years and, behind the Iron Curtain, several clubs have promised to threaten the West's domination.

At the start of 1974, only three clubs from Communist countries had won European trophies. Slovan Bratislava of Czechoslovakia took the Cup Winners' Cup in 1969 and, before British clubs took a six-year grip on the Fairs Cup and its UEFA equivalent, Ferencvaros (Hungary) and Dynamo Zagreb (Yugoslavia) took the Fairs Cup.

Yugoslavia have produced one of the most gifted sides ever to emerge from the Eastern bloc in Red Star Belgrade who gave a dazzling performance against Liverpool at Anfield in the European Cup in 1973 and thrilled television viewers.

The loss of Dragan Djazic, arguably the best orthodox left-winger in the world, to army conscription, has been balanced by the blossoming of Valery Petrovic, 19, a talented striker who has become a Yugoslavian idol. Behind Red Star's predatory attack are Krivokuca, a splendid overlapping full-back, and two magically creative midfield players, Bogicevic and Acimovic. The team has been created by the wise Milan Miljanic, who is an admirer of English football.

The only Russian team to reach a European final is Moscow Dynamo who had to suffer from the crudities of Rangers' supporters when they were beaten in the Cup Winners' Cup in Barcelona in 1972.

There are signs that the domestic domination of the big-city clubs of Moscow and Kiev is on the wane. Those of us who made the long journey with Tottenham to far-off Tbilisi realized with some surprise last year that a new force was emerging. Dynamo Tbilisi, from the Georgian capital, possessing a string of Russian internationals including Khurtsilava, the national captain, and Dzodzashvili, full-backs, Asiatiani, striker, and Givi and Levan Nodia, wing brothers, were described by Bill Nicholson, the Spurs manager as 'the best team we have met in Europe'. When one considers that the list of Spurs' European opponents over the years reads like a soccer Debrett, this was praise indeed.

It is evident that, all over Europe, if not the world, clubs are learning from their opponents and the days when overwhelming defeats for clubs from 'unfashionable' countries were the rule have passed.

# SOUTHAMPTON GATEWAY TO EUROPEAN FOOTBALL

## Fred Tyler,
Secretary of the Hampshire F.A., tells how
England's soccer link with France began.

## OXFORD

## CAMBRIDGE

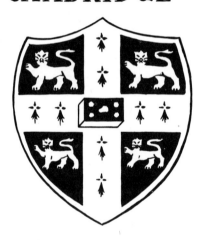

It all began about a century ago. A group of students from Oxford and Cambridge visited Le Havre and formed the renowned H.A.C. Sports Club. The trip was the forerunner of many sporting jaunts across the channel. It was also the first of a long series of exchanges which led ultimately to the 'twinning' of two famous seaports, Southampton and Le Havre.

Between the wars, Southampton F.C. and Hampshire F.A. teams maintained the soccer link with France. In those pre-jet days, of course, they made the trip by

80

ferry. In time various southern clubs began to make the crossing. Salisbury F.C. visited Turcoing and Paris, Pirelli General F.C. had matches against Le Havre, Cherbourg, and Rotterdam, while Netley Central Sports played the University of Paris. Other clubs were 'twinned', Basingstoke with Alencon, Winchester City with Versailles.

The great success of the annual Youth Festival held in Cannes in the south of France suggested to Pierre Crinierre, General Secretary of H.A.C., that a similar competition might be staged in Le Havre. Thus the first H.A.C. International Youth Tournament took place in 1969, Hampshire F.A. accepting the invitation to play. Among the players in that team were Steve Middleton, Wayne Talkes, and Paul Bennett, all of whom have since played First Division football at the Dell. Well-known teams to clash in that tournament included Calcio Brescia of Italy, Liege of Belgium, Ludvigshaven, and Leningrad.

William Forde, managing director of Pirelli General, presents the Tyro League Challenge Cup to former Irish international Tommy Traynor, general secretary of the Tyro League F.A.

The close bond which this first tournament created between H.A.C. and Hampshire F.A. meant that a series was bound to follow. In 1970, Thorneywood Athletic, a Notts County F.A. club which has boasted such top-class performers as Alan Birchenall, Tony Hateley, Henry Newton, and Peter Grummitt, took up the role of hosts.

Centenary Year 1972 proved a turning point. Another Youth Tournament was organized and this attracted more teams new to the concept of international youth football, including Morocco, Kladno of Czechoslovakia, and La Cahux de Fonds of Switzerland. A highlight of the centenary celebrations was the visit of the combined Oxford and Cambridge party under Professor Sir Harold Thomson.

It was after this important anniversary that the decision to introduce Under-13 and Under-15 international matches was taken. The first competition in the Centenary Year was between Le Havre, Caen, Portsmouth, and Southampton Tyro League. The Tyro League, incidentally, formed as recently as 1973 has had a phenomenal growth with membership now approaching 100 clubs.

Third Youth Inter-Port Tournament was held at Easter 1974 and it seems the series is here to stay. There are many ways in which links can be established between French and English soccer. Just as Southampton and Le Havre have been twin towns since 1973, could not the Saints and H.A.C. be twin clubs? After all Southampton is a gateway to the Continent.

Tommy Traynor (*centre, stripes*) nets a goal for the ex-Southampton professionals against Le Havre at the Dell.

# GET THIS!

Tony Matthews, West Bromwich Albion statistician, is prepared to bet that not too many readers have collected these items in their soccer archives.

In an away reserve match at Halifax in 1903 Darlington had two players sent off, not for offences against opponents, but for fighting each other! The culprits were Billy Smith and John Duffy.

Between 1929 and 1935 goalkeeper Tommy Poskett was with Grimsby Town, Lincoln City, and Notts County in that order, and all in turn were relegated.

Freddie Steele, when he was transferred from Mansfield Town to Port Vale in December 1951, became the first player-manager of a League side to change clubs.

Les Roberts, a Redditch lad, assisted no fewer than 16 League clubs between 1921 and 1936. In turn he played for Aston Villa, Chesterfield, Sheffield Wednesday, Bristol Rovers, Merthyr Town, Bournemouth, Swindon Town, Brentford, Bolton Wanderers, Manchester City, Exeter City, Crystal Palace, Chester, Rochdale, Rotherham United, and New Brighton.

Freddie Steele, first player-manager to change clubs.

Which Football League player broke a leg most often? Probably former full-back Albert Evans. He suffered five breaks during his playing days, three while with Aston Villa (1891–1907), one when with West Bromwich Albion (1907–08), and another while playing in a charity match in 1915.

Former Grimsby Town forward Jackie Bestall played for England just once, but when he did – against Ireland in 1935 – he set up three new records. Besides being the oldest at 33 to win a first cap, he was also the smallest at 5ft 2in, and the lightest at 9st 2lb.

When Luton Town became a professional organization in 1891, they paid their players 2s 6d (13 new pence) for a home match and 3s (15 new pence) when they played away.

George Male, the ex-Arsenal and England full-back, had quite a remarkable start and finish to his footballing career. In his first match for Arsenal in 1930 Blackpool were beaten 7–1, and in his last, in 1948, the Gunners clipped Grimsby 8–0. George made over 400 appearances for the club in those 18 years, including wartime games.

During season 1962–63 eleven Tottenham Hotspur players earned international caps. But all eleven never played together in the same Spurs team. They were: Greaves, Smith, Henry, and Norman for England; White, Brown, and Mackay for Scotland; Hopkins, Jones, and Medwin for Wales; and club-skipper Danny Blanchflower for Northern Ireland.

*Far left:* Former Arsenal and England full-back George Male

*Left:* Jackie Bestall, the oldest, smallest, and lightest player to win an England cap.

Ted Liddell is the only man in history who has held paid posts with seven different Football League clubs in the same city. He was half-back with Orient and Arsenal, manager of Fulham, assistant-manager of West Ham, and a scout with Chelsea, Tottenham Hotspur, and Brentford. Thus he served seven London clubs.

Stan Davis played for Preston, Everton, West Bromwich Albion, Birmingham, Cardiff, Rotherham, and Barnsley, in the 'twenties. He was a truly versatile player. At one time or another he filled all eleven positions. He also won 18 Welsh caps.

Willie Cook of Everton scored a penalty goal in three consecutive League games played over a period of four days in 1929, December 24, 26, and 27 – a Football League record.

Partick Thistle's goalkeeper saved no fewer than seven penalties while playing against Kilmarnock in October 1945. Each of his first six saves was ruled out by the referee who said that he had moved before the kick was taken. But the last save was allowed.

When defender Irving Rhodes netted from a free-kick for Rotherham United against Hartlepools in March 1937 he became the first full-back to score in his League debut.

Early in 1933, Alec Mackay, a goalkeeper (born 30 August 1913) was signed by Southport, his sixth Football League club. After he had played in one game for Southport he had tasted football in all four major Divisions and still hadn't reached the age of 20. His other clubs were: Wolverhampton, Hull City, Newcastle, Bolton, and Bournemouth – a Football League record.

On September 10, 1932 Halifax were leading Wrexham 2–0 with 15 minutes to play in a Third Division (N) match. The final score was Halifax 2 Wrexham 5, the most striking last quarter hour's transformation in Football League history.

On Saturday April 10, 1936 Swansea Town travelled 412 miles to Tyneside and played Newcastle United 24 hours after they had visited Plymouth Argyle, the longest distance ever covered by a team between Football League games on successive days.

Walsall fielded only eight players – seven regulars and a committee member – throughout a Second Division match at Darwen on December 26, 1894.

# DOWN THE LEAGUE AND PROUD OF IT

Alasdair Ross interviews
Roy Sproson, manager of
Port Vale, who says that good
football is not confined
to the First Division.

When it comes to life in soccer's lower regions few are better qualified to talk on the Third and Fourth Divisions than Roy Sproson, manager of Port Vale. Sproson, of course, was the man who all but eclipsed Jimmy Dickinson's record of 764 league games in his playing days with Port Vale. In fact he got within eight games of that all-time best total.

Does he regret not achieving football immortality?

'I honestly never let it worry me,' he says, 'although I suppose it would have been nice to beat Jimmy's record, I can't say I was upset when I finished with 756 league games behind me.

'Jimmy did a great job for Portsmouth and deserves that title. I reckon I might have passed the total though with ease, but for one season early in my playing career when I missed all but a few games because of ankle injury.'

Sproson called it a day at 41 at the end of the 1971–72 season with more than 800 first-team games to look back on and such experience certainly enables him to talk objectively on a footballer's life in the lower reaches of the Football League.

'The main point of difference,' explains Sproson, 'is that players from the Fourth and Third divisions don't earn the same kind of money as the boys in the top grade.

'I know a lot of people will think I'm being a bit cold-blooded talking in pounds and pence instead of straight soccer, but just like the First Division lads, the boys at the bottom are professionals.'

Sproson backs up his claim by recalling the plight of some Fourth Division players who struggle to make ends meet during the close season.

The player whose League record Roy Sproson nearly broke, Jimmy Dickinson who retired with 764 League appearances for Portsmouth. Sproson finished on 756.

'When I was playing I used to take a part-time job away from soccer in the summer months. We had a supporter who owned a dairy, so a few of us would take jobs as drivers with him on his milk floats. Other lads would work in the pottery industry around Stoke and Burslem. We had to work or go without.

'People expect footballers to be wealthy and most players like to keep up appearances with smart clothes and big cars. That takes money which brings me back to the point I'm trying to make. The top players are very well paid, whereas players in the lower divisions usually only earn better money when they win. Generally the one way they can add to their basic pay is by earning these bonuses. So with money at stake they all play that bit harder to win.

'You have less time to use the ball in the Fourth Division than in the First. The tackling is hard and the marking very tight. Only the skill factor conveys the difference between the two extremes.

'Don't forget that a lot of players who appeared in last season's F.A. Cup-Final for either Liverpool or Newcastle started in the lower divisions. Players like Kevin Keegan, Ray Clemence, Alec Lindsay, Terry McDermott, Pat Howard, and Malcolm MacDonald all began outside the big league and served their time in the Third or Fourth Divisions. A list like that underlines the immense playing potential which exists in the lower divisions. I'm never surprised when a Third Division club does well in the League or F.A. Cup.'

Sides like Swindon, QPR, and Aston Villa have all reached the League Cup-Final as Third Division clubs and Sproson himself was a member of that redoubtable Port Vale side which reached the semi-final of the F.A. Cup in 1954.

'That was the year we won the Third Division North championship. We'd beaten First Division sides Cardiff and Blackpool, the holders, before we played West Bromwich Albion in the semi. We lost – to a Ronnie Allen penalty. But that experience, along with many others, proves the point beyond doubt.'

In those days Sproson was an adventurous left-half, but he later switched to left-back. From there he moved to centre-half where he played out his career.

'There was only *one* place I could go after that, and that was goalkeeper!' he recalls with a chuckle.

Sproson as a player was promoted and relegated with a frequency that would upset many players, but he remained unperturbed throughout all these fluctuations. He now looks at soccer with a manager's eye and no doubt will go on as long in this new field as he did on it as a dedicated player.

'I loved every minute of my playing days,' he insists. 'It was all such good fun. The bad times were bad, but boy the good were fabulous. And you know that's the same in any division – if you care about the game.'

88

Getting up there with the ball, Roy Sproson (5) beats two defenders.

# STOP CHEATING— IT'S ONLY A GAME

says Jack Taylor,
World Cup-Final referee

THE END OF THE WORLD was the headline in one national newspaper. 'It's worse than losing a war,' declared Lord Wigg, 'a national crisis of the highest magnitude.' Of course, everyone connected with soccer knew what he meant. England had been defeated by Poland and were out of the final series of the 1974 World Cup.

Strange that people who can accept the adversities of this troubled world so much better than most nations should be so upset by the result of a game. But what is a game? The *Oxford Dictionary* describes it as a contest *bound by rules* and decided by skill, strength, or luck. To play the game, it says, is to *behave honourably*. The italics are mine.

As a Football League referee for 17 years and an international referee for 13 I have officiated in most of the football nations of the world. I am fully aware of changes in the game and the impact these changes have had at all levels of the game. I am also keenly aware that the demands placed upon the modern footballer are greater than ever before, indeed it is no longer playing or participating but winning that matters. This is largely because the financial rewards for winning have never been greater. With so much at stake, therefore, it is understandable that players have changed more than the game itself.

One of the most refreshing remarks of last year, for me, came from that colourful character, Bill Shankly. Asked what made Liverpool a great team, he replied, 'Keeping the game simple and playing for one another.' Of course, great sides need skill, ability, knowledge, and fitness, but without togetherness, that is teamwork, all the other qualities may be worthless.

Football is bound by rules which are simple enough but like so much else in the game they can appear to change by having a different interpretation placed upon them. We have come a long way from the days when the referee's job was to adjudicate the Laws of the Game. The operative word for today's referee is control, a word that does not appear in the rules.

Referees have always been criticized. Today's referees are said by many to compare unfavourably with the men of the recent past, men such as Jim Finney, Ken Dagnall, Kevin Howley, and Jack Kelly to name but a few. But I well remember that in their time they were sometimes compared unfavourably with the previous generation of referees – Reg Leafe, Arthur Ellis, and Jack Clough, for example. It will always be so. The perfect referee is not yet born and his mother has been dead a long time!

The task of the modern referee is more exacting than ever, as is the task of the players. And with the one-eyed monster, television, ever ready to analyse his split-second decision, he finds it hard indeed to avoid criticism. The slow motion replay, presented from different angles, can enable anyone at home to become an expert just by turning a knob.

In the highly professional field of top-class football authority cannot work without respect. Thus what the referee needs is co-operation from the players and they need co-operation from him.

People always talk more about the bad than the good and despite all we hear and read about cheating I don't think things are quite as bad as we are sometimes led to believe. We cannot pretend the cheat does not play his part. They are, in my opinion, in a minority but still far too numerous. I am convinced that the game is no dirtier than it has ever been. It is probably less physical now than at any other time. In fact it isn't usually the hard player that does the damage. By that I mean that the average fan calls him hard if he plays for our team and a hatchet man if he plays for the opposition.

What really has changed is the onset of petulant behaviour. This has been allowed to grow, thereby often creating poor entertainment for the most important person, the spectator. Why do players feign injury? Sometimes it is to get an opponent penalized, sometimes to allow trainers or managers to pass on advice, sometimes just to waste time. This kind of thing is far too prevalent and it was good to see that during the World Cup Finals in West Germany it was kept to a minimum, and the games were better for it. But again it can be difficult for a referee to decide just how serious an injury is. However, like most other spectators, I do find it rather disturbing to see a player reduced one moment to a pathetic heap of humanity, and then a moment later, after a splash of water, performing super-human feats of speed, stamina, and agility. Instead of receiving the enthusiastic applause of the crowd, such an obvious fraud should get the good old-fashioned bird, in my view.

As far as I am concerned, by far the worst thing that has happened and grown within the game is that ugliest of words and actions – *dissent*. It spreads like wildfire on the pitch and can certainly influence the many louts who disgrace soccer crowds in the guise of supporters of the game. Players will, of course, always appeal but appealing is not to be confused with open dissent, the open questioning of decisions accompanied by demonstrations of disgust while inviting team-mates to become involved in the argument. Any referee worth his salt must, having made a decision, stand by it. It disturbs me to see good players being lost to the game because of punishment for dissent. It is unnecessary and rotten for the game.

Another disturbing feature of the game today, a feature, in fact, of modern tactics, is the failure of players to retire a full ten yards at free-kicks. How petty it can look when highly intelligent players give the appearance of having no idea how far ten yards is. I have often wondered whether we could learn something from Rugby League where failure to retire ten yards can mean the ball being moved closer. But this again would probably give rise to new ruses on the part of the man who really wants to cheat.

Another nightmare for today's referee is that of foul or abusive language. The Laws lay down quite clearly that the player guilty of such language shall be sent off. But in a society which now has difficulty in defining foul or abusive language it is difficult to enforce this rule. Moreover some clubs allow players to express themselves freely during training which means that they carry through with the same sort of language in a match. In some games, were this rule applied rigidly, the playing area would begin to look short of players. Of course, no referee will tolerate foul language being used against an official. But we have come to accept that an expression of annoyance on, for example, missing an open goal, may be allowed to pass so long as it does not offend spectators.

It is a very old saying, but still a true one, that the game will always be greater than the individual. So let the few dissenters think again, particularly about the many youngsters who watch and copy and in whose hands tomorrow's world will lie. So please stop cheating – it's only a game.

Jack Taylor shows the yellow card to the Dutch team captain, Johan Cruyff, during the World Cup-Final in Munich.

CHARLIE GEORGE (ARSENAL)

94

TONY CURRIE (SHEFFIELD UNITED)

DAVID JOHNSON (IPSWICH TOWN)

96

PETER SHILTON (STOKE CITY)

# THE BEST OF BOTH WORLDS

## Tony Waiters

former England and Blackpool goal-keeper, talks about the satisfaction of a varied career in football

In 1967 at the age of 30 I hung up my boots. I had spent eight interesting years as the Blackpool goalkeeper and had picked up one or two honours on the way. Many people were surprised that I finished at such an early stage in my playing career – particularly when you consider that a goalkeeper often does not reach his peak until after 30 years of age.

The main reason for my decision was that I had already developed a deep interest in soccer coaching, and my ambition was eventually to move into management. I felt that being a goalkeeper imposed some limitations on gaining a full understanding of the game. I reasoned that it is one thing to see everything from behind the team, but very different actually to experience it as an outfield player. I am not trying to say that goalkeepers cannot become successful football managers. What I am saying is that playing at midfield, for example, should help to give a greater technical and tactical understanding.

I had thought about this at an early stage of my professional playing career and attempted to compensate for it. In 1960 I took the Football Association's Preliminary Coaching Award and then spent at least two afternoons a week for the next four years coaching in schools. With this practical experience behind me I went with Jimmy Armfield, my Blackpool team-mate and the former England captain, to the National Recreation Centre at Lilleshall where we both successfully com-

Tony Waiters in action in his Blackpool days.

pleted the Football Association's Full Coaching Award. In the next three years I stepped up the amount of coaching I was doing outside of normal club training hours. I worked with local teams, in schools, and on organized courses run by the Lancashire Football Association.

In training time at Blackpool I often played out of goal in five-a-side matches and occasionally in full games. This gave me a much better first-hand feeling and insight into outfield situations.

So in 1967 I left Blackpool and joined the full-time staff at the Football Association as their Regional Coach in the North West of England. For me this was an eye-opener. In the previous eight years I had viewed the game in many ways with blinkers on. Apart from my coaching experience, I had dedicated almost the whole of my life to improving myself as a goalkeeper. Everything else seemed of much lesser importance. My obsession with goalkeeping hindered me from studying other aspects of the game.

As the Football Association's soccer salesman in the North West it was necessary to make contact with people involved in football at all levels, from the Primary School level right through to the First Division. It opened my eyes. There was much on the administrative side of soccer which I didn't even realize existed. So it enabled me to look at football, even life, in a much broader way.

It was then my good fortune, in 1969, to be offered a coaching position at Liverpool. The next 18 months were probably the best I have spent in soccer to date. I felt that I was part of the most professional, the most enthusiastic, soccer club in this country, perhaps in the world. I say this without any disrespect to the other clubs with which I have been associated.

I think I surprised quite a few people when I returned to the playing side of the game at 33 years of age, joining Burnley from Liverpool as a player/coach in 1971. There were a number of reasons why I did this. One was that I had the greatest admiration for Burnley and I knew that in whatever capacity I was employed there I would gain a great deal of experience. Another reason was that I missed active match-involvement, and felt that I could still make a contribution on the field. The opportunity at Burnley enabled me to get the best of both worlds.

On reflection, the time I spent at Burnley was really of a stop-gap nature both for Burnley, who had serious goalkeeping injury problems, and for myself. I certainly knew that this was just a temporary phase before I moved towards club management. During the 18 months I was playing at Burnley I still attended the College of Technology in Blackburn to take a course in personnel management to further prepare myself for football management.

Eighteen months after going to Burnley a chance to return to full-time coaching

100

Waiters saves for Burnley. Attacker is England of Tottenham Hotspur.

took me to Coventry City where I became their Chief Coach. Unfortunately the experience wasn't a lasting one as I resigned following the circumstances of the dismissal of Noel Cantwell, the Peterborough United Manager. It was still a rewarding experience and certainly the four months working with Noel and Ian St John, who was Assistant Manager, were in no way wasted.

After a month out of work Ronnie Yeats asked me to assist him at Tranmere until the end of the season in 1972. Big Ron had just taken over as Player/Manager at Tranmere and wanted me to give him a hand while he got the organization in order. It was my first real insight into Third Division football and once again my eyes were opened. Third Division football is fiercely competitive, well organized, and much more physical – in the best sense of the word – than in the First or Second Division.

At the end of that season Tranmere offered me the position of Assistant Manager but I felt the time had most certainly come for me to attempt to move into a top job.

Thus I returned to Southport to work on the beach as a Lifeguard – a job I had done for a number of years in my early 20s. As you can imagine it was a paid holiday and a wonderful relaxation prior to taking without doubt the hardest job in soccer, that of manager. Not that I had a club to go to. That was the gamble that I had taken when I left Tranmere.

Fortunately Ron Suart, the Assistant Manager at Chelsea Football Club, who had originally signed me at Blackpool when he was Manager, offered me the opportunity of scouting for Chelsea on a part-time basis. Chelsea sent me to watch a game at Plymouth and this coincidence led me eventually to take the Manager's job there.

In my first year of club management I also held the position of Manager/Coach to the England Youth Team. This imposed an additional strain through having to do two jobs at the same time. However it did allow me to see something of football management at international level. Even better, while I was the England Youth Team Manager we won the 'Little World Cup' held that year in Italy. In the team were players such as Ray Hankin of Burnley, Glen Keeley and John Peddelty of Ipswich, Barry Siddall of Bolton, Stephen Powell of Derby County – all players who have established themselves as young stars of today and probably even bigger stars of tomorrow.

Many people still ask me if having been a goalkeeper hindered me in my career as a football manager. I would say not. But remember I am only in my first two years in management. What I have already learned is that the Football Manager must be Jack of all trades *and* master of most – or fail.

102

# A FOOTBALLER'S MOST PRIZED POSSESSION

## by Dr Neil Phillips,
### former physician to the England team

A football player's talents revolve around his feet, so it is very surprising how few footballers give proper care and attention to their feet.

Most people wash their hands four or five times a day, but washing their feet is, by comparison, a special event. It is a fact, however, that the feet should be thoroughly washed twice daily, and properly dried after each washing, especially between the toes where water tends to collect. Dampness predisposes the skin to infection, particularly the infection called Athletes Foot, so thorough drying of the feet after washing is essential. When the feet have been dried, they should be well powdered with a good talcum powder, and clean, well-fitting socks worn daily.

In general, women's feet are subject to more abnormalities than men's. This is mainly due to the fact that women usually wear high-heeled shoes. Recent men's fashion has produced platform shoes and these have become very popular among our trendy football players. The constant use of platform shoes can produce the same foot abnormalities in men as are seen in women. Therefore, if platform or high-heeled shoes are worn, it is essential that the heel-base within the shoe is horizontal to the ground, and not at an angle. A flat heel-base prevents the foot sliding forward and avoids the whole foot being forcibly wedged into the toe of the shoe with each walking step. It is better, of course, not to wear platform shoes. Everyday shoes should be chosen carefully, be of a good quality, and well-fitting.

Most footballers get a thrill out of obtaining a new pair of boots. Apart, obviously, from having good quality boots, which fit well, new football boots should always be 'broken in' over a period of time. The new boots should be used initially for short periods in training, and their usage gradually increased until they can be comfortably worn for the period of a match. There is no excuse for wearing a pair of unworn boots in a match, and hobbling about after half-an-hour because the boots do not fit properly or because they have not softened, and are rubbing against the skin of the feet and causing blisters.

Some people's feet are subject to excessive sweating, and this gives rise to the very unpleasant odour of 'sweaty feet'. This excessive sweating is called hyperhidrosis, and the skin on the sole of the foot becomes red, macerated, and tender. Persons subjected to sweaty feet, should wash, dry and powder their feet frequently each day, avoid rubber-soled shoes, wear thin clean socks daily and use sandals for footwear instead of shoes. In severe cases of hyperhidrosis, under medical super-vision, the soaking of feet in a 3 per cent formalin solution for 15 minutes each evening is very effective in drying up the sweat, preventing excessive sweating, and thus curing the condition.

Few people, footballers included, are familiar with the correct method of cutting toenails. Unlike fingernails, which are cut in a rounded-off fashion, and shaped to the end of the fingers, toenails should be cut straight across, so that the sides of the nail are almost over the ends of the toe. If toenails are cut in this manner, the danger of developing in-growing toenails is much reduced.

Blisters occur commonly on the feet during the pre-season training period, and should be given immediate treatment. The skin over and surrounding the blister should be cleaned with an antiseptic lotion, and one side of the blister pricked with a sterile needle. A gauze pad is then placed over the blister, and gentle pressure applied to squeeze out the fluid within the blister. A sterile dressing is then applied over the blister.

Athletes Foot is an extremely common skin condition, caused by a fungus which affects the skin between the toes and the sole of the foot. At first, there is some itching between the toes, the skin thickens, becomes white and sodden-looking, and coarse scales occur on the sole of the foot. The infection is spread by the common use of baths, showers, and bath mats. Players should dry their feet thoroughly after washing, particularly in between the toes, and report at once if they develop any skin irritation or eruptions. The towels and socks used by infected players, should be kept apart from the other players' kit. The regular and persistent use of anti-fungicidal powders will generally clear up the condition, although it may recur from time to time. At least two or three applications of the powder are needed every day, and in addition to the powdering of the feet, socks and the inside of shoes should also be powdered. This treatment may have to be con-tinued for several weeks, or even months in some cases. In persistent cases, the Doctor may prescribe an oral antibiotic called Griseofulvin, and this usually clears persistent cases.

# YE OLDE ENGLISH SOCCER

Some quaint glimpses of in the Middle Ages as revealed by contemporary literature.

Every phase of social life in England has its literature illustrating the influence of each particular aspect upon the life of the people through the generations. Sport also has its literature, but football, to a considerable extent, has been neglected since very few writers of eminence have used it as a main theme. There has, however, been a change within living memory and today novels, plays and films catering for adults are replacing the 'hero-thrillers' of the 'Boys' Own Paper' type of story that we all enjoyed in our youth.

Prior to the Elizabethan age, the game of football is mentioned only in official documents such as the Acts of Parliament of 1314, 1349, 1389 and 1401 which contained injunctions to suppress 'such idle practices', or in casual comment by historians. With very few exceptions this tendency to inveigh against the game pervaded the literature of the 16th century, notably in Sir Thomas Elyot's *Boke, called the Governour* with its condemnation of 'footeballe wherein is nothing but

105

beastlie furie and exstreme violence whereof procedeth hurte and consequently rancour and malice do remain with them that be wounded, whereof it is to be put in perpetual silence'. Elyot, indeed, had a courtly hatred of anything energetic, and especially if it is related to the activities of what he considered to be the lower classes. He could never have brought himself to say as did Barclay in 1508 in his *Fifth Eclogue*:

> 'The sturdie plowman, lustie, strong and bold,
> Overcometh the winter with driving the foote-ball,
> Forgetting labour and many a grievous fall.'

Even with the Golden Age, sport was rarely made the subject of eulogy. The dramatists, with the few oft-quoted extracts from *King Lear* (Act I, Scene 4), and the *Comedy of Errors* (Act II) apart, ignored football even in reference, and in the more sedate literature of the times, the trend to pass strictures on any form of amusement incompatible with a meek and chastened spirit that, as with Stubbes, awaited the end of the world, was paramount. As a Puritan this author of the *Anatome of Abuses in the Realme of England*, objected to every kind of sport, not only for itself, but because it was played on Sundays: 'Lord, remove these exercises from the Sabaoth. Any exercise which withdraweth from godliness, either upon the Sabaoth or any other day, is wicked and to be forbidden'. He had a particular and violent objection to football . . . tennis and bowls were 'fooleries' but football was a 'devilishe pastime'. Stubbes, according to many reviewers, had played the football which was a 'friendlie kinde of fyghte', and there is internal evidence in his writing that he knew many of the tricks whereby 'whosoever escapeth away the best goeth not scot free, but is either forewounded, craised or bruised'.

Even the King, James I, in his *Basilikon Doron, or Manual of Precepts for his Son and Successor* made a reservation. He praises some sports as good for the body but 'from this count, I debar all rough and violent exercise, as the football, meeter for laming than for making able the users thereof'. As the King copied many of his 'sentiments' from Thomas Elyot, it is very likely that his views on football were merely borrowed and not original.

Burton, in his *Anatomie of Melancholy* (early 17th century) mentions football as being one of the general recreations of the country folk, and there is ample evidence that, at this period, it was usual to play sport after dinner on Sunday and 'Some do toss the light and windy ball aloft with hand and foote'.

106

In his *Table Book*, Hone quotes a description of London in 1634 by Sir W. Davenant:

> I would now make a safe retreat, but I am stopped by one of your heroic games called foot-ball; which I conceive (under your favour) not very conveniently civil in the streets, especially in such irregular and narrow roads as Crooked Lane. Yet it argues your courage, much like your military pastime of throwing at cocks, since you have long allowed these two valiant exercises in the streets.

The period of the Civil War and the Cromwellian Protectorate were short in actual years, but the effect of the supremacy of Puritanism was profound. Except possibly in London, it not only put a stop to Sunday football, but it made the game less acceptable on other days. In earlier days, football was a national game, although not accepted in court circles; from 1650, however, there was a slow but steady decline in the popularity of the game as a sport for men, and this persisted for nearly two hundred years, indeed, until an athletic revival in the middle of the 18th century. Its lost place in general esteem, despite a development in the schools, accounts for but odd references in standard literature and a dearth even of comment on the game. True, Pepys records that on January 2, 1665, during the great frost, 'the streets were full of footballs', but the inference is that the apprentice-lads kicked these about to keep warm. The adult population had more vital matters to consider, at any rate in London if we judge the age by contemporary lampoons:

> They're mounted high; contemn the humble play
>   Of trap or football on a holiday
> In Fines-bury fieldes. No; 'tis their brave intent
>   Wisely t'advise the King and Parliament.

Strangely enough, although Charles II, the Merrie Monarch, was a great patron of athletic sport, and certainly gave his patronage to football matches arranged between his retainers and those of his noblemen, this fact is not brought out in the literature of the later 17th century, and it is from a French author, M. Misson, who published his *Memoires et Observations faites par un Voyageur* in Paris in 1698 that the most interesting comment is found:

En hiver le Footbal est un exercice utile et charmont. C'est un balon de cuir, gros comme le tête et rempli de vent; cela se balotte avec le pied dans les rues par celui qui le peut attraper; il n'y a point d'autre science.

This extract shows the change from the 'devilishe' practices of the times of Stubbes for the game he described was neither 'utile' nor 'charmant'. Misson is the link between the old rough-and-tumble of mob football and the more disciplined game which was being developed in the Schools.

This change of attitude is further exemplified by the one reference made to the game in the *Spectator*, in one of the Sir Roger de Coverley papers. In this, Addison, adopting the role of a West Country correspondent, describes a 'Country Wake, being the eve-feast of the Dedication of our Church'. As usual there is a touch of patronage in his style . . . the courtly Londoner deigning to mix with country-folk (at Bath), but it did recall his schooldays at Charterhouse, evidently, it would seem, that away from London, the 'upper classes' took part in the athletic sports of the 'lower classes' when given a chance.

I was diverted from a further observation of the cudgel-players by a football match which was on the other side of the green, when Tom Short behaved himself so well that most people seemed to agree it was impossible that he should remain a bachelor until the next wake. Having played many a match myself, I could have looked longer on the sport had I not observed a country girl.

108

LEIGHTON JAMES (BURNLEY)

STEVE PERRYMAN (TOTTENHAM HOTSPUR)

PHIL PARKES (QUEEN'S PARK RANGERS)

TREVOR BROOKING (WEST HAM UNITED)

112

# THOSE VITAL MOMENTS

By Newcastle United striker
## Malcolm Macdonald

Goals make soccer's turnstiles click. They are what the game is all about. As a striker, goals are my business and I realize only too well that I'm in the entertainment business. The trouble is goals aren't always easy to come by. You have to graft really hard for most of them. But you can improve your chances of scoring if you have the skill, experience, and knowledge to exploit the vital moments that come in every match.

Yes, the vital moments when to head for goal and crush your opponents. And you can gamble that those vital moments will come just before and after the half-time break or within the last quarter of an hour of a match. During those periods of play it pays to sharpen up your senses so that you can detect the slightest lapse of concentration or sign of tiredness in the opposition. Once you spot a weakness you must pounce upon it, and go hell-bent for goal.

Just take a look at the goal statistics. You will find that more goals are scored in the second half than the first, and that a lot of goals come shortly before or immediately after the interval. A recent survey of the timing of goals in League football showed that very few were scored in the first 15 minutes.

That's not really surprising to me. It's my experience that defences play much more tightly than they used to do, and more teams are making cautious starts. Generally it is thought unwise to risk conceding an early goal by going flat out from the start. Teams size each other up in the first quarter of an hour and consequently the game is usually a stalemate in that period with very few goals being scored.

Nevertheless the opening minutes are often vital and do have a bearing upon the rest of the match. It's like a game of chess. If you make the right moves and assess correctly the strengths and weaknesses of your opponent, you can go a long way towards winning.

The opening gambits do count. You should be able to spot whether the defender marking you is a strong left- or right-sided tackler, whether he lies deep in defence or comes in quickly at you. You may discover that if you run wide to his left, he is struggling to catch you. Then you must play upon the weakness, and use your skill to take full advantage of your knowledge.

As goals are at such a premium early on in a match, it gives me a great kick if I can pop one in. A quick goal can unsettle a defence. Sometimes it will demoralize a team completely. But my theory is that if you do grab an early goal, you must go on attacking. One goal ahead after five minutes . . . that's fine. But I'd rather be two goals up in 10 minutes.

Some teams fall back in defence if they do manage to get an early goal. Often that leads to their own downfall. They allow the other side to take the initiative

114

(*Above*) Another one in the net and Malcolm Macdonald exults.

and eventually their heavily battered defence breaks down.

My policy is attack. Obviously it is stupid to throw everything at the opposition before you have worked out where and when to launch your assaults effectively.

That survey also showed that on average the first goal comes in the 31st minute of a match. I find that easy to understand because the concentration of a player can start to crack after half an hour's tense, probing football. These lapses of concentration often come just before the half-time whistle and often let in goals. It seems to me an awful lot of goals are scored in the last five minutes of the first half.

That's the period of the game when some players start to listen for the welcome whistle that will bring relief to aching limbs. You may be nursing a slight injury and can barely wait to get off for some quick treatment from your trainer or physiotherapist.

So quite naturally some footballers are not at full stretch as the game gets towards half-time. If you can sense that one or two of your opponents are starting to flag or likely to lose concentration momentarily, you must strike for goal and strike quickly with all the force you can muster.

If you do snatch a 44th-minute goal, it works wonders in the dressing-room. Not only are your team-mates elated and full of half-time cheer but also it causes utter consternation in the enemy camp. You can be sure there are some hot words flying around in the other dressing-room, accusations, and recriminations. 'Why did you let him . . .' 'What were you thinking of . . .' Those are the sort of questions sparked off by your vital goal.

But whatever you do, don't relax and start basking in the glory of your first-half goal. You must remember that the time is ripe for another. Grit your teeth and come out fighting for the second round. You may have ruffled the feathers of your opponents in the first half. Now is the time for all good strikers to come to the aid of their side. You must go all out to flatten them with a snap goal as soon as the game resumes.

Lots of games enter the final 15 minutes with the scores level or with one team only one goal ahead. And lots of games have been decided in the dying minutes by players who have kept alert and fought off morale-sapping thoughts of tiredness.

Take my tip. It's knowing when to score them that counts – in those vital moments that often become golden.

(*Opposite page*) Malcolm Macdonald moved from Luton to Newcastle United to earn the name 'Supermac' for his goalscoring flair.

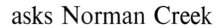

# WHAT HAPPENED TO THE OLD 1–2–3–5 FORMATION?

## asks Norman Creek
### former England amateur international.

Whenever we old football fanatics get together after a particularly frustrating match which has probably ended in a goal-less – and often a soul-less – draw, it is a hundred to one that some nostalgic comparison will be made with the so-called 'good old days'. Ex-players, especially those of pre-war vintage, will glibly assure all those within hearing that soccer reached its zenith when the five forwards played in a line.

Looking back through their rose-tinted spectacles, our senior citizens proclaim that the years between the two Great Wars were the golden age of the game. They lay the blame for the mediocrity of many modern matches on the shoulders of team managers and coaches who have encouraged their players to conform to a series of numerical formations. Not so long ago, such numbers as 4–2–4, 4–3–3 and 4–4–2 were meaningless gibberish to the average spectator. Today, the mass media have brought the jargon right into the forefront of our tactical talks.

There is obviously a limit to how far we can go back if we wish to compare the old with the new, in football or in any other game. Arguments as to whether Grace was a greater cricketer than Bradman, Vivian Woodward a more accomplished centre-forward than Tommy Lawton, or whether Harry Vardon's golf was superior to that of Jack Nicklaus – all these and dozens of similar comparisons must be seen in the light of conditions at the particular time.

118

What fun it would be today to watch a side like the Old Etonians of a hundred years ago playing soccer with a goalkeeper, two men 'out' and eight men dribbling and charging round the field with the ball at their feet. It would certainly be fun, but it would allow little comparison or parallel with the game as it is played today.

Making allowances for the differing conditions such as modern improvements in football boots and dress – not to mention the ball itself – would the game today be a better one if we returned to the old formations? There is no denying that the fundamental cause of all complaints about the modern game is the 'safety first' approach. This attitude, though, is by no means confined to soccer. Bowlers who are content at cricket to control batsmen, tennis players who are quite happy to keep the rallies going, rugger forwards who refuse to risk letting the ball out – all these are no better than the footballer who, immediately he receives the ball, looks round for a colleague to whom he can pass it. All these may be highly-efficient performers, but they are all so very dull to watch.

This unfortunate modern attitude stems from fear of making mistakes. In soccer especially there is so much at stake in most of our League matches, Cup-ties, and international games that our players, at all levels, are often hesitant to take on an opponent. During the past twenty years, we have inherited two unfortunate legacies from our friends on the continent, the hugging and pampering of goal-scorers, and maintaining possession of the ball at all costs. The theory of possession play is perfectly sound and simple: so long as we enjoy a monopoly of the ball, our opponents cannot possibly score. So, once we have taken the lead, we stall and delay.

So we were bound to come back sooner or later to the problem of the wing-forward in our modern game. It is he who, by doing the disappearing trick, has reduced the old forwards to a meagre three, or even to a microscopic pair. Yet it is only fair to point out that the much-vaunted five forwards of bygone years never really played in a straight line across the field. Even in those days, at least one of the two insides would play a few yards behind his four colleagues and act as a link with his half-backs and defenders.

Alex James, for example, was a forward who rarely scored a goal – in his finest season he notched one solitary goal – but he saw to it that his club wingers, Cliff Bastin and Joe Hulme, more than made up for that deficiency, the one often scoring from a centre by the other.

This reciprocity between wingers was one of the most attractive features of the old five-man forward line and, because the lack of it is so obvious, it is particularly lamented by critics today. When Sir Alf Ramsey made the brilliant discovery that the area of the playing pitch within ten or twelve yards of each touchline could be

119

utilized by such outstanding men as Wilson, Cohen, Ball, Peters, and Hurst – although none of them was an orthodox winger – he was able to strengthen his 1966 World Cup defence without really weakening his attack. The immediate result was a glorious success. But how sad it is today to see clubs at every level of the game trying to emulate that plan with players who have few of the necessary qualifications to carry it out. Voices are heard appealing for 'old-fashioned wingers', but their effect is minimal.

I am not one of those die-hards who believes that five genuine forwards would solve all our problems today. As a matter of fact, a forward line of my playing era, even if it consisted of Sammy Crooks, David Jack, Dixie Dean, Jimmy Seed, and Jimmy Ruffell would, I am convinced, fail to live up to their reputations if they had to play against a First Division team today, for the simple reason that they would so rarely be able to retain possession of the ball. They were positive players who were prepared to take risks, whereas their modern counterparts are largely safety-first performers.

In those days between the two World Wars, the 'numbers' game had not been invented, of course; we never thought of playing 2–3–5. If such an expression had been in use then, I suppose it would have been fair to say that we played a 3–3–4

Former Wolves manager, Stan Cullis, one of the past masters who does not like comparing modern players with those of the past.

formation with the 'stopper' or 'policeman' centre-half between the two backs, and with one inside-forward lying behind his other forwards and between the two wing-halves. Yet even in those far off days we were, perhaps unintentionally, strengthening our defence at the expense of our attack.

I played at centre-forward once in a full England trial between two of the greatest constructive insides of that time, Kelly of Burnley and Seed of Tottenham. They were so skilful that whenever they wished, they could use me as a decoy. They interpassed behind me, across my front, and occasionally even over my head! We were never a fine forward line that afternoon. The pitch was frozen but I managed to be up in the six-yard area to score the only goal of the match off my bottom as I slithered helplessly forward. Yet even that act of jugglery failed to convince the selectors to give me a cap that year!

Talking about international caps, it seemed a sound idea to obtain the views on this subject of such past masters as Ted Drake, Tom Finney, Stan Cullis, and

Nat Lofthouse, Bolton and England centre-forward during the 1950s.

Stanley Matthews and Tom Finney, wingers who 'created a spectacle on the field that excited spectators and players alike'.

Nat Lofthouse. Between them they played for England on 124 occasions and their careers spanned a period of 25 years from 1935 to 1960.

Drake says: 'I would always go for two fast wingers and a centre-forward. From the point of view of attraction I feel we should go back to the old 1–2–3–5 formation. I feel that the centre-forward would probably prefer that.' Drake feels that we are thinking too much in the negative at the moment and that the old game was a much better spectacle for the public. 'We must always think of the game as an attraction,' he says.

Tom Finney, perhaps the most accomplished winger of them all, says: 'I firmly believe that wing men have a key role to play in modern football. It is becoming increasingly difficult to find or make openings through the middle, and more thought will have to be given to the idea of wing men as the answer to the ultra-defensive systems we encounter in today's game.'

Stan Cullis who, of course, went on to become a famous and experienced manager when his playing days were finished, says 'I dislike the exercise of comparing present-day players with players of a bygone era, along with the comparison of tactics, because opinions on both are mostly hypothetical, difficult to prove, and equally difficult to disprove. The old tactics of having a centre-forward and two wingers, with both inside-forwards playing behind these three forwards, had a similarity with present-day formations, but the terms "strikers" and "midfield players" have blurred the analogy. As a centre-half, I did not have another defender holding my hand to reassure me with extra cover for any mistakes I made. When we are told how important it is to have players with the speed and skill to get behind this modern defensive wall, it amazes old-fashioned people like myself why we apparently do not breed wingers who can do this.'

Nat Lofthouse, England's centre-forward during the 1950s would also like to see the modern game improved as a spectacle. Nat ways: 'In my view, the present formations do not encourage a positive approach to the game. I would not enjoy playing today. I would certainly miss the flair and attacking spirit of wingers like Tom Finney and Stan Matthews. The orthodox wingers of my day created a spectacle on the field that excited spectators and players alike. The skills of the orthodox wingers are available to the game today, if only they could be exploited.'

In view of all these criticisms, most of which I feel are fair comment, dare I assert that I have occasionally seen genuine signs during the past season of managers and coaches utilizing that deserted strip of the pitch within eight or ten yards of the touch-line? One winger, at least, is now regarded as expedient if not essential to a team. If only he could be transfigured into a second Tom Finney, the 1970s might produce a team formation worthy of comparison with that of the good old days.

# THE DEVELOPING NATIONS

How soccer is putting down roots in four nations where the game's popularity is beginning to advance.

There can be very few places left in the world where soccer is unknown. There are now over 140 countries in membership with FIFA, football's 'United Nations'. The game spread from the British Isles to Europe at the turn of the century, it soon caught on in South America, and now is widely played in Asia, Africa, Australia, and New Zealand.

U.S.A.

In recent times progress has also been made in Canada and the United States but the tremendous appeal of baseball and ice-hockey has made the task of those trying to spread the game of soccer in the States very difficult. However, many more men play now than a few years back and the fact that it is in the colleges and high schools where most interest has been aroused, augurs well for the future.

Boston on the eastern seaboard is one city where good progress has been made. The Boston area youth soccer league has at least 125 boys' teams and 12 girls' teams. Some idea of the interest may be obtained when it is recalled that when the league began in 1969 with 8 teams – spectacular growth by any criterion.

The name John O. Best will be remembered by older football supporters as an outstanding referee in the States. Here is his report of the Thomas Dewar Cup for the year 1973. It provides an entertaining and colourful account of soccer as seen through the eyes of an American:

It was warm, sunny and a clear, beautiful day in Los Angeles on June 10. A day for relaxation, picnics, the beach or just enjoying a Sunday with the family. For many in the Los Angeles area it was just that, but not for those supporters

124

of the Maccabee S.C. team, nor for the visiting eleven representing Cleveland's pride, the Inter-Italian S.C.

The divisional finalists were to meet in the Grand Final of the U.S. Open Cup that afternoon. The Western Champion and the Eastern Champion meeting for the right and honour to hold and defend the oldest soccer trophy in the United States. This trophy, the symbol of soccer supremacy, was given to this country by Sir Thomas Dewar of Scotland in 1914. Held in possession by some of the greatest teams developed on these shores: Bethlehem Stell of Pennsylvania, Ponta Delgada of Massachusetts, Greek-Americans of New York, Kutis of St Louis, the Los Angeles Kickers, and last year's champion, the Elisabeth Sport Clubs of New Jersey.

The long climb to the Grand Finals had now reached the summit. The glory was to the victor, but the hard ascent to the peak had its rewards and would always remind the runner-up of their outstanding and successful run for the Cup.

The road for Inter had been blocked all the way by opponents who were strong and determined to be finalists and to win. At home in Ohio, the Ukrainian Americans and Croatian Zagreb, who knew the Inter eleven as well as they knew themselves, were determined to be the victors. But Inter overcame their resistance and moved on to the first round proper to defeat Inter-Hope of Rochester.

Each game became more of a challenge, as it should. Opposition included Canonsburg of Pittsburgh and the Philadelphia Ukrainians, the latter a club with a great history, winning the Dewar Cup in 1960 and 1961 and repeating again in 1966.

However, 1973 was not the Philadelphia team's year. Inter won 3–0, to go on to the divisional final against the awesome Greek Americans of New York City.

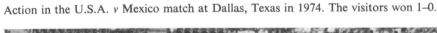

Action in the U.S.A. *v* Mexico match at Dallas, Texas in 1974. The visitors won 1–0.

Three-time champions, from 1967 through 1969, and once again making a serious run for the Cup they were a great team with confidence and ability, and the desire to win. As Inter made believers out of the Ukrainians in Philadelphia, so they did with the Greeks in New York. For, when the Final whistle blew, the score was 3–1 and Inter were on their way to the Grand Final.

A great record had been achieved, twenty-three goals scored and but five conceded in Cup play, an average of 3.8 for and a mere 0.8 against.

Just as impressive was the Western Finalist. Having defeated four excellent opponents in the California South grouping, they looked forward to the inter-state play. First it was Croatia S.C., then St Stephens, and the Los Angeles Gauchos before meeting the San Pedro Yugoslav Americans in the state finals, the same San Pedro team, who were finalists in 1971 and again in 1972.

When the game ended the Maccabee team moved on by virtue of a 1–0 victory to meet the San Jose Portuguese in the divisional semi-finals. Meanwhile the Chicago Croatian's were moving toward the divisional final with victories over the Bravarian S.C. of Milwaukee and the Denver Kickers of Colorado. Maccabee 2, San Jose 0, was the result of their game. A week later the Chicago eleven was to feel the sting of defeat by a score of 1–0. This grand finalist from the West is not noted for scoring, with only six goals in their last five cup games, but a stonewall on defence. No one in those final five games dented the nets against this superior team. Here was the classic contest. The unstoppable offence; Inter-Italian of Cleveland with a 3.8 goalscoring average, versus the unmovable defence; Maccabee of Los Angeles, with a zero against average in their final five cup contests.

The match was one of the finest games played in the West in a long time. Inter-Italian began attacking right from the opening whistle, playing delightful football at a very fast pace. However, it was Maccabee who hit the net first. A penalty shot awarded for a tripping foul in the 13th minute of the game. Inter evened the score during a concentrated attack at the 35th minute, but Maccabee, though playing their fine defensive game, broke away and scored their second goal at the 41-minute mark. Thus ended the first half, a real scorcher, with Maccabee leading 2–1.

Thirty minutes into the second half, Inter tied up the game with a lovely goal and this score held until the final whistle despite the fact that the Inter team were playing with only ten men, one player having been ejected early in the second half of play. Overtime, and at the eight-minute mark, Jim McMillan the Inter centre forward secured the go-ahead goal and it looked like it was all over for the Los Angeles team. Less than two minutes later, Maccabee's substitute

126

Yarone Schnitman put the ball in the Inter net and the score was once again tied. This gave the Maccabee new life and they dominated the balance of the overtime period, scoring two more goals, one by Schnitman and the other by UCLA star Fesseha Emanuel.

Thus it ended. Maccabee 5, Inter-Italian 3. The Dewar Cup has found a new home for 1973. Once again it has moved to the Far West. Not since 1964 has it been past the Mississippi River, but now it resides with a well deserved champion, and it may be there for a long time to come.

Another American soccer legislator is Matthew Boxer. He has this to say:

The decision of the national convention to place youth soccer development under the jurisdiction of a separate vice-president has had a magnificent response. In about a year, the number of youth players jumped from 14,000 to nearly 32,000. These figures represent only youth players actually registered in all youth categories the numbers rose from 25,000 to 125,000 in just over 18 months.

Incidentally, the national association changed its name in 1973 from United States Soccer Football Association to United States Soccer Federation.

NEW ZEALAND

New Zealand soccer is enjoying an unprecedented period of growth. Gone are the days when the game was regarded as a 'cissies' game played only by emmigrants. Twenty-eight per cent of the population rose from their beds in the early hours of the morning to watch the F.A. Cup-Final between Leeds United and Sunderland, beamed upon their TV screens by satellite and the result was spread across the headlines of the National Sunday Newspapers. The game's phenomenal growth owes much to the screening of English League and Cup games on TV. These games have captured the interest of even the most ardent Rugby Union and League supporters.

The New Zealand Football Association has met the challenge of maintaining the growing public interest by the formation of a National League of ten clubs spread throughout the major cities of the North and South Island. This has been an ambitious step forward considering the country is the size of the British Isles with a mere three million population. Costs to each National League club have been high due to the need for air travel but generous sponsorship, especially by the Rothman's Sports Foundation, has enabled the competition to prosper.

Although the numbers of Kiwis playing soccer continues to grow the expatriate influence is still strong especially among the coaches of the top clubs. Ken

Iran's goalkeeper, Mansur Rashidi, makes a spectacular save in one of the pre-World Cup matches against New Zealand at Newmarket Park, Auckland.

Amstrong the ex-Chelsea and England wing-half of the 'fifties is the coach of the powerful Mount Wellington team who are the present holders of the Chatham Cup, the New Zealand equivalent of the F.A. Cup. Ken has two of his sons playing in the team. Bert Ormond, brother of the Scottish team boss, is coach to Blackhouse Bay, another of the top clubs based in Auckland and like Ken he has two of his sons playing for him.

Last season the National League was won by Christchurch United under the coaching of Jerry Conley who had a spell as youth coach to Preston North End two seasons ago. This was the first time since the League's formation, four seasons ago, that the leadership was wrested from Auckland clubs.

With the recent introduction of a national pre-season cup competition under the sponsorship of Air New Zealand to supplement the National League and the Chatham Cup it is obvious that, in New Zealand, soccer is the name of the up-and-coming game.

128

AUSTRALIA

Mr Mike Laing, an F.A. coach, who knows the football scene in Australia, writes:

While the interest is rapidly growing at a junior level, there are many problems still to overcome at senior level. Surprisingly, for a country with such a large land mass, there is a shortage of grounds and suitable training areas. For example, at the club I coached in the First Division of the N.S.W. league, we operated, like all the other clubs, three teams. We had a first and second team plus an under-18 team, all of which played on the same pitch on the same day, with the first game commencing at a quarter to twelve on Sunday, immediately followed by the second team game. So at three o'clock your first team go out on to what can be a very difficult and well-used surface, especially if it has been a wet weekend. On the Saturday three rugby teams will also have played their three matches on the self same pitch! A young player who had returned to Australia after a year with Leeds United commented that, while he had learned a great deal from his time spent with Leeds, it would be difficult for him to reproduce the skills and techniques he had learned owing to this problem of ground conditions.

This, however, is not the case with all the clubs. Indeed, the National team have a very fine stadium and playing surface, with good floodlighting, praised by Gordon Banks who played there in 1973 during Stoke City's tour of Australia.

Other touring teams that year from England were Birmingham City and F.C. Bournemouth, all of whom thoroughly enjoyed their end-of-season tour and the generous hospitality which welcomed them throughout the tour.

All Australian competitions are organized within their own state. This is rather a pity as I feel that greater interest would be produced if they had a National League. Last season gates were averaging only around the 2,000 mark for league matches, but a marked increase was shown on games at State level.

However, this could be quite difficult to introduce now, as most players have transferred inter-state to N.S.W., where they can enjoy a higher standard of soccer, and the cash rewards are much higher. Most First Division sides operate with a semi-professional staff of around 25 players who train three evenings a week and are well paid for the time and effort spent. I would compare their wages with those of the average English Third Division side. The money is made available from the splendid social clubs that promote soccer activities.

Quite a number of players are imported from the U.K. but the Australian Soccer Federation are now considering putting a limit on the importation of players. This step would greatly assist in the development and building of the

National team from Australian-born players a move, which would, quite rightly, gain tremendous support.

Geographically, Australia has a problem in gaining experience at international level. However their tremendous achievement in reaching the finals of the World Cup in Munich will be of great benefit to them.

## NORWAY

George Curtis sends us this report:

The Norges Fotballforbund (Norwegian F.A.) was founded in 1902 and from modest beginnings now embraces no less than 5,115 teams within 1,313 clubs, representing approximately 300,000 players, an impressive figure drawn from a nation with a population of less than 4,000,000. Throughout the 31 counties, schools football competitions are active and only economic problems prevent inter-county encounters. For the young under-18 football aspirants, the annual Norway Cup Competition is the tip of their football iceberg. Clubs throughout Europe enter. No less than 800 clubs took part when Sir Stanley Rous, President of FIFA, opened the 1973 tournament in which the lads from Consett, Co. Durham, lost on penalties in the Final against Tistadalens Turn F.C. (Norway).

The Norges Fotballforbunds coaching scheme, built on similar lines to the Football Association scheme with it's qualification standards, is well established and progressive in its outlook. Schoolteachers are particularly encouraged to attend courses and so are more able to spread the football gospel to these young charges.

Professionalism has not yet reached these shores. Players' ambitions are to represent their country at all levels and they are completely fulfilled when, after 25 full international selections, they are presented with the traditional gold watch, suitably inscribed, by the NFF President.

From the Island of Sualboro, very close to the North Pole, to Kristiansand in the South, the Norwegian Football Association controls the game. The League consists of seven Divisions and competition is keen as clubs strive for promotion. The 12 clubs forming the First Division enjoy gates of between 3,000 and 12,000 spectators. Playing standards are good and, in the European competitions,

Against a backdrop of snow-covered peaks, soccer in full swing in Norway's polar region at Svalbard.

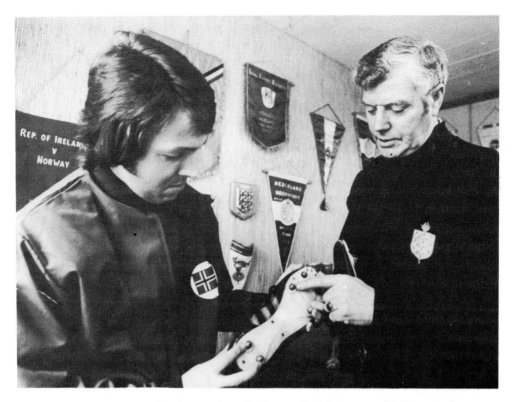

F.A. Staff Coach, George Curtis, examines the 'ice stud' with Arve Mokkelbost, Assistant Director of Coaching at the Norwegian Fotbollbund.

players raise their game to command respect from their professional opponents.

The Cup-Final is played late in October and ends the season which begins in April. The King of Norway, King Olav V, presents the Trophy in front of 25,000 spectators in Oslo. Then 'King Winter' takes over, bringing snow and ice in abundance.

But players defy the elements and after a brief close-season, start their next season's preparation as early as mid-December. Threading pointed metal studs into the soles of their football boots, they play practice games on snow and ice surfaces. Standards of play are excellent. It is literally football on ice!

Norway's footballers accept the fact that football is a teaching game and seek knowledge to improve. If it is true to say that I have seen higher playing standards in other countries blessed with more favourable training elements – not least climatical conditions – it is also true to say that in terms of dedication, Norway's footballers are second to none.

131

# THE GOLDEN YEARS

## Roy Peskett

recalls the days when the reputations
of the great League Clubs were built

When, during the last century, football became organized within the bounds of control and discipline, records had to be kept of the history of the game. These records, highlighting the successes and disappointments of clubs and players, are fascinating to study. Some of the clubs had their golden years in the very early days, before the turn of the century, yet are still well remembered round the world.

In the modern era clubs enjoy opportunities for international success and players diaries may read: Saturday, Highbury; Wednesday, Moscow; Saturday, Newcastle. But who can say or argue whether a League title in 1894, in those early exploratory days, was a better or worse achievement than success in the 1970's

Let us look back to the days of the billycock hat and tasselled cap. Currently successful teams like Leeds United, Manchester United, or Liverpool did not figure prominently in those early days. In the beginning there were Aston Villa, Blackburn Rovers, and Newcastle United. Others made a temporary mark.

Now Blackburn Rovers struggle in the Third Division. But time was when the famous blue and white halved shirts won the Football Association Challenge Trophy three times in succession. That was in 1884–86, and when they completed the hat-trick, the F.A. gave them a special trophy in perpetuity. Rovers also won the Cup in 1890 and 1891, but perhaps the season of 1882 was the most memorable to the people who figured in it. Not only did they finish runners-up in the Cup, but they also went 35 consecutive matches before being beaten!

Proud Preston, so nicknamed because of their record at the time, also had their greatest era in those first formative days. They won the first-ever First Division championship in the birth-year of the Football League, 1888–89. By winning the F.A. Cup the same year (for the second year in succession) they became the first

The Aston Villa team which won the Cup and League 'double' in 1896–97.
*Back row:* G. B. Ramsay (Secretary), J. Grierson (Trainer), H. Spencer, J. Whitehouse,
J. Margeschis (Chairman), A. Evans, J. Crabtree, T. Lees (Director), C. Johnstone (Director).
*Front row:* Dr V. Jones (Director), James Cowan, C. Athersmith, J. Campbell, J. Devey
(Captain), F. Wheldon, John Cowan, J. Reynolds, F. W. Rinder (Director).

team in professional English football to bring off the F.A. Cup and League
'double'. It has only been done by three teams since then.

Preston, who still wear the letters P.P. on their club badge, did the 'double' in
a manner which I say is unlikely to be equalled. They did not lose a League game
nor concede a single Cup goal!

By establishing themselves as one of the leading teams in those years running
up to the turn of the century, Aston Villa indelibly wrote themselves into football
history, and into the hearts of young football followers ever since. Dennis Shaw
has written more about Villa elsewhere in this book.

Bury has been overwhelmed in the modern era as the giants of Lancashire have
collected trophies and left Bury and some of its neighbours far behind. But until
there is an avalanche of goals at Wembley, no one can take away the unique
record they have held since 1903. In that year's F.A. Cup-Final they defeated

133

Derby County 6–0 at the Crystal Palace, a record win for a Final. In their only other Crystal Palace appearance they beat Southampton 4–0.

Sunderland have briefly came back into the limelight from time to time. These were Wembley Cup wins in Coronation Year, 1937, and again as a Second Division team in 1973. But the greater majority of their illustrious records were set up before the First World War. In the ten years between 1892 and 1902, they won the League title four times and were runners-up three times. They also won it in the season before the War and again in the middle 'thirties in the days of Carter, Gallacher, and Gurney.

There has always been great rivalry between Roker and Newcastle, and there was great rejoicing in Sunderland when in 1908 Sunderland set up their record away win, 9–1, at St James's Park. But Newcastle went on to win the First Division title the same year. It was Newcastle who continued the dominance of the North East in the early years of this century. The famous black and white Magpie shirts won the League title in 1905, 1907 and 1909. The following year they lifted the F.A. Cup.

Then, in the sparkling 'fifties, when there were quite a lot of good teams about, Newcastle made Wembley their regular calling spot by winning the F.A. Cup in 1951, 1952 and 1955. It says much for the versatility of their players that only three of them figured in the three winning teams in five years, Jackie Milburn, Bobby Mitchell, and Bobby Cowell.

It is sad to see Huddersfield Town languishing in the Third Division when you remember that they were the first team to achieve the almost impossible feat of winning the First Division title in three successive years, which they did between 1923 and 1926. They very nearly went nap. In season 1926–27, Huddersfield finished runners-up, five points behind Newcastle, and the following year only two points behind champions Everton.

Charlton's great sprawling white elephant ground in South East London once rang to cheers and adulation from huge crowds. I was present before the Second World War when 76,000 packed the Valley for a Cup replay with Villa. But it was in the years on either side of this War which were their greatest. In 1934–35 they won the Third Division South title. The following season they continued the climb into the First Division as runners-up, and in the following season finished only three points behind the champions, Manchester City. In the first year of the resumed F.A. Cup, after the War, Charlton lost to Derby County in the Cup-Final, after extra time, and the next year went even one better by beating Burnley.

Portsmouth had two tremendous years in the early 'fifties after having held the F.A. Cup throughout the War by virtue of beating the hot favourites, Wolves, in

Part of Arsenal's amazing pre-war record was a second F.A. Cup win in 1936. In this action picture, Sheffield United's goalkeeper, Smith, is seen keeping the score down to 1–0.

the last peacetime Final. Then in season 1948–49, fifty years after their formation in the Southern League, Portsmouth won the First Division title amid almost universal jubilation. The following year they did it again.

Arsenal became only the second team in modern years to do the 'double', which they did in 1971 as we can all easily remember. But their greatest spell, and possibly the most tremendous by any club in the Football League, came in the 'thirties.

Look at this amazing record: 1930, F.A. Cup winners; 1931, League champions with record points (66) and goals (127); 1932, Runners-up in League and Cup; 1933, 1934, 1935 League champions; 1936, F.A. Cup winners; 1937, third in League; 1938, League champions; 1939, fifth in League.

It was then that Arsenal became the most famous team in the world, and their fame has never died, even though the Halls of Highbury do not ring with quite so much triumph these days. Their players, including James, Jack, Hapgood, Drake, Copping, Hulme, Bastin, Male, and Roberts gained 140 international caps between them in that fabulous golden era.

JOHANN CRUYFF (NETHERLANDS)

DRAGAN DZAJIC (YUGOSLAVIA)

GERD MÜLLER (WEST GERMANY)

ANDRZEJ SZARMACH (POLAND)

# MANCHESTER UNITED– THE GREAT YEARS

The story of how a great club's fortunes rose to
a climax in the 'fifties.
reproduced from *Manchester United*, by Percy M. Young.

In 1955 two important appointments were made at Manchester United. Jimmy Murphy became Assistant Manager with particular responsibility for the younger players; a sparking unit of gaiety and high seriousness, with the echo of the Rhondda in his voice, and with ample experience of football with West Bromwich Albion and Wales. Les Olive became Assistant Secretary. An effective former junior goalkeeper, also capable of filling any vacant position in emergency, he had a flair for administration and public relations. Such appointments stemmed from the general policy and their final justification, if such was needed, came in 1958.

On the material side, the notable addition, after the rehabilitation of the main buildings on the ground, was flood lighting. The lights, set on high pylons, of which three of the four stood outside the ground itself, were ready in time for the Bolton match of March 25, 1957 – in which year Murphy was appointed Manager of the Welsh national side. The floodlights have since that time illuminated many great occasions, but it is to be observed that before such aids were introduced they had been installed on the practice ground in 1950, so that the young players and amateurs on the Club's books could benefit from evening training.

In the 1949–50 season, United won neither League Championship (in which they were again runners-up – this time to Portsmouth) nor Cup, but they continued to play the same imaginative and scientific football. Aston, Cockburn and Pearson were members of the England team against Scotland, and Carey – who played at inside-right again when Delaney was absent – was elected 'Sportsman of the Year'. Johnny Morris went to Derby County at a then record fee of £24,000, and Johnny

140

Architects of Manchester United's greatness, Matt Busby (*above*) and (*overleaf*) his Assistant
Manager, Jimmy Murphy.

Jim Murphy.

142

Downie, former Bevin boy and a native of Scotland, was signed from Bradford Park Avenue.

The Semi-Final of the Cup furnished one of the heroic episodes in the tapestry of great deeds. By 1949 the Wolves had become the arch-enemy, as in the past had been Aston Villa, so that they were greeted in Manchester at the beginning of the 1948–49 season, thus: 'Few teams have proved such consistent attractions over the years as Wolverhampton Wanderers . . . Their encounters with United were usually of cup-tie flavour . . .' When a collision between the clubs in the F.A. Cup occurred, nothing was beyond sensational possibility; especially as this, by some curious chance was the first such encounter.

The prelude to the occasion was the season's League record between the two clubs. Here, on goals, the United held a slender advantage, being able to set a 2–0 win at home against a 2–3 defeat at Molineux. The Semi-Final was played at Hillsborough; a dramatic game in which it would have been an injustice if either side had lost. A certain partiality prompts the gloss that had Wolves lost it would have been a greater injustice, for they played much of the match with only nine fit players. The replay was on Everton's ground; the result a 1–0 win for Wolves by the narrowest of margins. Five minutes before full-time Jesse Pye, from what many outside of Wolverhampton considered an off-side position, crossed the ball to Sammy Smyth who scored with a neat turn of the head.

During the summer the neighbouring Manchester City lost by retirement Frank Swift, later tragically, to be associated with the United, and prepared for another calamitous season ending with relegation yet again. In December the United, prudently looking to the future, signed Ray Wood of Darlington, ultimately to succeed Jack Crompton's successor Reg Allen, who had come with glowing credentials from Queen's Park Rangers. A bright start to the season – eight games without defeat – was not sustained, and before the last match victory over Fulham, there was a sequence of nine games without a win. Warner's illness and an injury to Carey were, perhaps, partly responsible; but the period was one of frustration in which the ball, as they say, seldom ran kindly. Nevertheless, the team finished the season in fourth place, and the eyes of the wise were concentrated on the promise of the 17-year-old Whitefoot, Jones, Jacky Blanchflower, Birkett and Viollet, and the scarcely older McNulty, Redman, Birch, and Byrne, in the Central League. Whitefoot made his first appearance in the senior side against Portsmouth on April 5.

Scarcely had the season ended before the United were away to America in the *Queen Mary*, to be greeted at their hotel in West 46th Street by a cheerful banner which proclaimed 'Welcome to the great Manchester United Soccer Team'.

Frank Swift, Manchester City's immortal goalkeeper who died in the Munich air disaster.

144

Among the more interesting matches of a strenuous tour were those against Besiktas, champions of Turkey, and the *American Soccer League Team.* Victory against the former was hardly won, by 2–1, but in the latter the United, winning by 9–2, exhibited the perfect classical model. The Captain of the U.S.A. team at that time was an expatriate from Wrexham, who had taken the unusual step of signing for Philadelphia Nationals. Eddie McIlvenny enjoyed the experience during that summer of embarrassing his fellow countrymen by leading the U.S.A. to victory against England in the World Cup at Belo Horizonte. He was, considered Busby, too good for Philadelphia, so he came to Manchester, where, however, he enjoyed less fame than in America. The American tour had other consequences, for Charlie Mitten, like the City pilgrims of 1894, was lured by the wealth of the New World to throw in his lot with the soon-to-be notorious Bogota. Mitten was soon disillusioned, but he never returned to the United. The memory retained of America and Canada by the United party was entirely favourable, and three years later another was undertaken, losing only two matches out of twelve, to Tottenham.

Before the 1950–51 season commenced the United paid one of their periodic visits to Scotland, to play a friendly match with Aberdeen. Recalling the Charity Shield match of 1948, in which they allowed Arsenal to gain a 3–0 lead in eight minutes, they gave Aberdeen a start of three goals. Unlike the Arsenal match which was finally lost by 4–3, after a stirring revival, this resulted in victory for the visitors by 5–3. In November, Jimmy Delaney, closely followed by Tommy Bogan and Tommy Lowrie, went back to play for Aberdeen, for by now the young men were knocking imperiously on the door.

On October 7, Redman (20 years of age) and Mark Jones (17) played, not without distinction, in the side that defeated Sheffield Wednesday by 3–1 at Old Trafford. Aston and Chilton were away on that day on international duty, and Cockburn was injured. Thus the long-playing McGlen, who like Chilton, had been wounded during the war, was moved to left-half from left-back to accommodate Redman. This match gave a splendid opportunity to the United supporters to appreciate how much was owed to Carey at right full-back.

With a player like Froggatt to keep under observation and two new colts to see through their teething troubles, he nevertheless found time to dive through to Allen's rescue when Allen himself had given up hopes, and yet keep an eye on the general direction of strategy in his own forward line.'

In mid-summer Busby made a more dramatic positional change. Rowley was unfit and Aston, who started his MUJAC career as an inside-forward, took over at centre-forward. When Rowley recovered, he reverted to his earlier station at outside-left. The conclusion of this experiment was Aston's quite brilliant collection

145

of 15 goals, *plus* one in a cup-tie. At a later point in the season, Aston returned to left-back and Rowley to centre-forward, while Roger Byrne was moved to the left wing from full-back. Yet again the team completed the season as runners-up, for the fourth time in five seasons, this time four points behind the Spurs. In the reserve side two players, there for the first time, especially impressed; Geoffrey Bent, captain of the Salford School Boys' Team that won the England Schools' Trophy, and Ronnie Cope, from Crewe, a Schoolboy International centre-half.

The year 1951 was marked by the Festival of Britain. Football made its contribution both on the international and the national level. At Old Trafford, a match of more than ordinary interest was staged, between the United (without Carey who was playing for Eire against Argentina) and the Red Star of Yugoslavia. The result was a 1–1 draw.

When the United dropped to fourth place in the League, supporters with short memories were disappointed, but the following year the Championship was gained. Almost half a century earlier a sanguine writer had prophesied: 'Should the United get into the First League, they will speedily become one of the richest and most powerful clubs in the competition.' In 1952 the prophecy was amply fulfilled. It was, however, no walkover. At times during the season, half-a-dozen clubs were in the lead, any one of them looking for a time like potential champions.

From Christmas onward it looked as though Arsenal, undefeated from December 29 until April 21, would emerge not only as Cup winners but also League Champions. The 'double' however, remained as inaccessible as ever. Arsenal lost to Newcastle in the Final, having conceded the League to the United at Old Trafford on April 26. If Arsenal had won that match by a margin of 7–0 they might still have gained one of the two major awards, but with Ray Daniel absent through injury and his deputy sustaining a broken arm in the match, they had no chance. The United were irresistible and won tumultuously by 6–1, demonstrating all the basic skills, and showing also that few teams 'can make use of them with quite the same aplomb as the United'.

The team on that day was: Allen; McNulty, Aston; Carey, Chilton, Cockburn; Berry, Downie, Rowley, Pearson, Byrne.

In the course of its history, Manchester United has enjoyed the services of a number of captains of great character, integrity, and distinction. Black, Powell, Roberts, and Carey stand out as those who have contributed most to the Club, and to football in general in this capacity. To the professional side of the game they brought the qualities noted elsewhere in such as Lord Kinnaird, and in the disposition of their gifts demonstrated a point not without its social significance. Carey, the most modern of the great captains of the United, was an all-round man.

146

In the course of his long active career, he played in practically every position in the team at one time or another. He spent his leisure in the acquisition of such knowledge as would stand him in good stead in later days, gaining, incidentally a very fair working knowledge of modern languages. He joined the British forces during the war, not because he had to (he was a citizen of Eire), but because he felt an obligation to the community which had given him opportunity. At the end of the 1952–53 season he retired, to take over the managership of Blackburn Rovers. Having rehabilitated Blackburn, restoring them to the First Division, he went to Everton.

The Championship side of 1952 contained much experience, but in some players the fires were beginning to burn low. The next three seasons saw the growth of a new team, the main link with the old being Allenby Chilton, who took over the captaincy from Carey. The need for new talent was apparent at the beginning of the 1952–53 season, for by the middle of October the team was paired at the foot of the table with Manchester City. Tommy Taylor was transferred from Barnsley for a fee of nearly £30,000 (the effect of which may be noted on the balance sheet). He, the most compulsive centre-forward of his era and withal one of the most modest, was one factor in the team's ultimate rise to eighth place. Other names began to make news.

Duncan Edwards, a native of Dudley in Worcestershire, schoolboy International, captain of the United Youth Team, honoured by the Lancashire F.A. as an inside-forward, came into the side at sixteen years of age, on April 4, 1953. It was a characteristically unostentatious entry on the occasion of a disturbing defeat by Cardiff by 4–1. Edwards, soon to dominate every game in which he played with an authority greater than any shown by so young a player before, passed his initiation test. Skipper Johnny Carey, taking a rest from the team said 'He's a good 'un – the best I've seen for his age'.

At the end of the season, Dennis Viollet made his first appearance in the first team at outside-right, and at St James' Park, against Newcastle United. That match deserves notice for another reason. In December, Jack Crompton had fractured a cheek-bone against Chelsea (Carey took over in goal and the United managed to hold on and win). Further goalkeeping casualties left the team without a regular player in that position by the beginning of April. In January, admiration, admittedly with a little generous envy, had been freely expressed for Gerula, the goalkeeper whose exertions were largely responsible for Walthamstow Avenue's sensational draw in the third round of the F.A. Cup. Les Olive, the assistant secretary, keeping active by assisting and directing the junior teams, in which he played in numerous positions, was therefore called out of his office and put on to

147

Matt Busby pictured with half-back Duncan Edwards in 1957.

the Newcastle train with instructions to keep goal the following day. Appearing as an amateur, and in a state of understandable apprehension, he performed his duties effectively if not spectacularly. The game ended in a 2–2 draw. That exemplifies team spirit, and the interdependence of players and the officers at Old Trafford. Besides Edwards and Viollet, there were also Lewis and Pegg who went from junior football to the First Division in 1952–53.

As for the youth teams, they were carrying all before them: their spoils included the Championship of the Manchester, Manchester Amateur, and Altrincham Service of Youth Leagues, the Gilgryst Cup, the Altrincham F.A. Junior Cup and the F.A. Youth Cup. In the latter competition – to be won by the United five times in succession – the opposition was provided by Wolves, who lost on aggregate by 4–8. The successful United team was: Clayton; Fulton, Kennedy; Colman, Cope, Edwards; McFarlane, Doherty, Lewis, Pegg, Scanlon.

Fulton, Colman, Doherty, Lewis, and Scanlon were all former Manchester or Salford schoolboy players.

In the succeeding seasons, the young players of the United continued to overlord it in their various spheres of activity. In 1954, appearing on a larger stage, they won an International Youth Tournament in Switzerland. The next year the Club occupied second place in the Central League, and won its Championship again in 1956.

Despite comparative inexperience and necessary changes in personnel, the first team managed to stay in the hierarchy in 1954 (at the end of which season Stan Pearson quietly migrated to Bury) and in 1955. To finish fourth and fifth in these seasons was, indeed, a magnificent achievement. Emphasis has, rightly, been placed on youth, but the young men of Old Trafford would be the first to observe that youth needs guidance. On January 3, 1956, a tribute was paid to seniority, for on that day a television set was presented to the Club's chairman, Mr H. P. Hardman 'in token of his work for the Club over 40 years'.

Although Tommy Taylor was unavailable at the beginning of the 1955–56 season the United began well. On October 29 victory at Cardiff took them to the top of the table. A moderate spell in the next six weeks or so found them not quite invincible, but by Christmas they took complete control of the situation. Henceforth, they were unassailable, and their championship success, for the second time since the war, was assured after beating Blackpool at Old Trafford on April 7. The gates were closed half an hour before the kick-off with 60,000 crammed into the ground. Blackpool scored first and held a 1–0 lead at halftime. Afterwards the United forwards became demoniac, and the Blackpool defence was helpless. Two goals – the first a penalty – by Berry and Taylor were no representation of an

Winners of the Football League First Division in 1955–56, Manchester United were runners-up in the F.A. Cup-Final.

*Back row:* E. Colman, W. Whelan, M. Jones, R. Wood, I. Greaves, D. Edwards.
*Front row:* J. Berry, R. Byrne, D. Viollet, T. Taylor, D. Pegg.    *Inset:* J. Doherty.

immense superiority. Despite Matthews's right-wing probings and occasional well-times passes, Ray Wood in the United goal had a generally restful afternoon. The youngest team in the League, and unbeaten at home, finally stood clear of all rivals by the enormous margin of eleven points. In that year attendances at football matches generally decreased. Of the few clubs able to point to an increase Manchester United were one.

By now the twin policies of nurturing young players and inculcating adaptability were paying the most handsome dividends, most of all because virtually every first team position was duplicated. Apart from the fact that this developed intense individual keenness, it was an insurance against the numerous calls made on the Club by representative sides. In the 1920s and '30s there were times when it was impossible to release club players for international matches. Now this was no longer the case. Byrne, Edwards, and Taylor played for England against Ireland in October 1956, while Jackie Blanchflower was at centre-half in the Irish side. Whelan played for Eire against Denmark; Clayton and Colman were called up for the Army side, from which Charlton was only absent on account of injury. Practically every player in the United team was a star in his own right. Even so, there were those who were convinced that the best of Manchester United was still to come. Bernard Joy, the old Arsenal player, stated in the *Star* one evening in the autumn of 1956, that the as yet unbeaten United needed another three or four years to mature. By then, he said, they would be 'strong claimants for the unofficial title of greatest English club side of all time'.

In the League during the 1956–57 season the United imperiously brushed aside all opposition, completing the season, with only six defeats, eight points ahead of 'Spurs. In the F.A. Cup the Final round was reached by preliminary victories over Hartlepools, Wrexham, Everton, Bournemouth, and Birmingham City. In these the most meritorious opponents were the least notable, Hartlepools and Bournemouth, who each only lost by a single goal.

The Cup-Final against Aston Villa was one of a series that in recent years have been won and lost fortuitously. After eight minutes' play, Ray Wood was injured – a fractured cheek-bone – and the United were compelled to move Blanchflower into goal, where he played splendidly for the greater part of the game. Ten men and a positional change that so upset the balance of a finely-adjusted mechanism was too great a handicap, particularly against an opposition of the commando-like ferocity of Aston Villa. Villa were not a great side, but, on their day, very difficult to overcome, and in McParland they possessed one of the best match-winning forwards in contemporary football. In the second half McParland scored two well-timed goals.

152

The 1957 F.A. Cup-Final at Wembley, Tommy Taylor heads home a corner from Duncan Edwards in the last minutes of the game to make the score 2–1. But Aston Villa won the Cup, and Manchester United had to wait until 1963 to recapture the Cup which they had not won since 1948.

The match, however, was not yet quite over. With seven minutes left Taylor headed a goal from a corner by Edwards. Wood, who had intermittently appeared on the right-wing, went back into goal, and Roger Byrne, a great captain on this occasion, called up his men for a last effort. Whelan, in fact, penetrated the Villa goal, but it was disallowed because of a previous infringement. The hour-glass emptied with the United still pressing for equality. Again the double capture of League and Cup proved unattainable. The Cup-Final teams were:

Aston Villa: Sims; Lynn, Aldis; Crowther, Dugdale, Saward; Smith, Sewall, Myerscough, Dixon, McParland.

Manchester United: Wood; Foulkes, Byrne; Colman, Blanchflower, Edwards; Berry, Whelan, Taylor, Charlton, Pegg.

This, however, was not all in that climactic year. During previous seasons the reputation of Manchester United had become international. On November 11, 1952, for instance, the Club had been invited to Antwerp to play against Austria F.C. as a memorial to the lately deceased John Langenus, an international referee held in universal respect. When, therefore, in 1956, the Club were invited to participate in the European Cup Competition, inaugurated by the French sporting journal *L'Equipe*, there was general satisfaction, except at League headquarters, where doubts were expressed as to whether engagement in the tournament would adversely affect the English League. Reasonably enough, it was pointed out that an English side undertaking such a commitment would possibly need to play sixty matches in the course of a season. The United (who in fact played fifty-seven games that year) reviewed the situation, and decided to add the European Cup to their other commitments.

In the First Round the United met the Belgian champions, Anderlecht. In Belgium they won 2–0. There being no flood-lighting at Old Trafford then, the return match was staged at Maine Road on September 26. It was a wet night, but the United were unperturbed. They played to perfection, giving, perhaps, the finest exhibition ever displayed by a United team. In the memories of those who were there this stands out as a piece for the 'Golden Treasury' of football. The United won by 10–0; 4 goals by Viollet, 3 by Taylor, 2 by Whelan, and 1 by Berry. On this match the Belgium captain, Jeff Mermans commented: 'After they had scored their sixth goal against us they still ran as hard as they had at the start. We had played against the crack teams of Hungary and Russia – and never been beaten like this. Why don't they pick this team for England?'

In November came the Second Round matches against the West German team

A shot from United's Taylor is tipped over the bar by Villa goalkeeper Sims in the 1957 Cup-Final.

Borussia from Dortmund. At Old Trafford a stern, even match gave the United a 3–2 win, a slender margin with which to travel. On an intensely cold night – so cold that Ray Wood kept his track suit trousers tucked into his stockings – two defences stood impregnable. By virtue of the 0–0 draw United went forward, thus commended by Alfred Preisler, captain of Borussia: 'In England they swamped us in the first half with incredible football. In Germany they fought like tigers. They will win the European Cup.'

In January the team travelled to Bilbao, in Spain, where on a muddy ground and swept by a snow-storm they quickly found themselves three goals in arrears. By an effort the United came up to 2–3, but a Bilbao renascence extended the margin to 2–5. Then, late in the game, Whelan pirouetted through the Spanish defences to score a brilliant final goal. The match was lost, but the impression left by the team with the Spaniards was indelible. The ambassadorial virtues of the team were described gratefully by the British Consul, in a report to the Foreign Secretary. A communication from the Foreign Office to the Club incorporating this report is one of the treasures of Old Trafford. Athletic Bilbao came to Manchester on February 6, 1957. In yet another fantastic evening at Maine Road the United surged to a 3–0 victory, the last goal came only six minutes from full-time. Three days later the team gave their answer to those critics who opined such exertions were too much by beating Arsenal by 6–2. The *mot juste* for the games was provided by the Bilbao captain – Piru Gainza: 'Magnifico. With a two goal lead from Bilbao we thought we had them. But they played with such passion in Manchester that we were overwhelmed.' Passion: an overflow from the vocabulary of art. But Manchester United creates artists.

In the Semi-Final the United lost to Real Madrid, before 130,000 spectators in Madrid, and drew at Old Trafford, the flood-lights now being available, 2–2. Such was the end of a great adventure. For Manchester the abiding memory was the Bilbao visit, which produced the most exciting match ever witnessed in the city.

That the United team of 1957 was great is inescapable, even though the secret of greatness is finally unfathomable. Some part of it, however, is revealed by two of its architects. Matt Busby answering the question, 'What makes a Manchester United footballer?' said: 'I give you the answer in three words: skill, fitness, character, and the greatest of these is – character.' Roger Byrne added his footnote: 'One of the secrets of Manchester United's success is that nearly all of us grew up together as boy footballers. We were knitted into a football family. Apart from Johnny Berry – formerly with Birmingham City, Tommy Taylor, and Ray Wood, who quickly fitted into the Old Trafford set-up – the Manchester United way is the only way we know.'

# THE A-Z OF ENGLISH SOCCER HISTORY

A chance for you to learn about some of the
forgotten facts of English soccer history
and to help us collect some more

Every corner of this land of ours, each county, city, and village, has contributed to the story of English football. In the following alphabetical list landmarks in the game's history are mingled with not-so-well familiar episodes. There are, of course, many many more historic events and the F.A. would like to hear from readers of local incidents or facts which can be published in the next edition of the book. They should be sent to The Publications Department, The Football Association, 16 Lancaster Gate, London W2 3LW.

**ACCRINGTON** Accrington Stanley F.C. was one of the original members of the Football League when it was founded in 1888. The club was disbanded in 1962.

**ALDERSHOT** Two players were killed by lightning during the Army Cup-Final in 1948.

**ASHBOURNE** Shrove Tuesday football has been played in the streets since the Middle Ages.

**ASHINGTON** Jack and Bobby Charlton's birthplace. The brothers were in the successful England World Cup team of 1966.

**BARNSLEY** The present Football League club was founded in 1887 by the Curate of St Peters Church, Barnsley.

**BERWICK** Berwick Rangers F.C. are the only English team which plays in Scotland.

**BIRMINGHAM** In 1895 the original F.A. Cup was stolen from a shop window in Birmingham. Aston Villa were holders of the Cup at the time. The second F.A. Cup was subsequently replaced by the present Trophy, which was won for the first time in 1911 by Bradford City.

**BOLTON** The present club was founded in 1874 as Christ Church F.C.

One of the worst disasters in football history occurred at Bolton Wanderers ground at Burnden Park in 1946 when 33 people were killed and hundreds injured at an F.A. Cup Tie.

**BLACKBURN** Blackburn Rovers F.C. won the F.A. Cup in three consecutive seasons between 1884 and 1886.

**BRADFORD** Albert Geldard, 15, became the youngest player in a Football League match when he appeared for Bradford Park Avenue against Millwall on September 16, 1929.

**CAMBRIDGE** The first rules of football known as the 'Cambridge Rules' were formulated at Trinity College, Cambridge, and pasted up at Parker's Piece.

**CARDIFF** Cardiff City F.C. became the only club to take the F.A. Cup out of England when they were winners in 1927.

**CHARTERHOUSE** Famous Public School in Godalming, Surrey, where football has been played from the earliest days.

**CHIPPENHAM** A bare-footed player from India startled spectators in match played here in 1922.

**CLAPHAM COMMON** Clapham Rovers F.C., winners of the F.A. Cup in 1880 played Association and Rugby football on alternate Saturdays in the 1870's.

**CLAPTON** Clapton F.C. were one of the first teams to play football on the Continent – at Antwerp in 1890.

**CORNWALL** A game called 'hurling at goales' was played in the county in the 16th and 17th centuries.

**CRADLEY HEATH** Birthplace of Stephen Bloomer, England International forward, who played for Derby County.

**CRYSTAL PALACE** King George V was the first reigning monarch to attend an F.A. Cup-Final when he was present at the Burnley v Liverpool match in 1914.

**CUMBERLAND** Steel workers from Sheffield introduced the game to West Cumberland.

**DARWEN** The Lancashire F.A. was formed here in 1871.

**EAST ANGLIA** A game called 'kicking camp' was played in East Anglia in the 17th and 18th centuries.

**EAST SURREY** The East Surrey Regiment was concerned in a famous action in the First World War on July 1, 1916, when an advance was made on the German lines by 8th Battalion 'kicking footballs before them'. The footballs are preserved at the Regiment's Museum.

**EVERTON** The present Club played in the Lancashire Junior Cup prior to 1887.

**EXETER** Football was played at St Lukes College, Exeter, for over a century. The first County match was played in Devon at Exeter in 1888.

**FOREST, LEYTONSTONE** One of the Original entries in the F.A. Cup in 1871–72.

**HANLEY** Birthplace of Stanley Matthews, the first professional footballer to be knighted. He will probably be remembered for all time as England's most famous player, who continued playing to his 50th birthday.

**HITCHIN** Location of a Football Museum.

**HUDDERSFIELD** Huddersfield Town F.C. won the Football League Championship in three consecutive seasons from 1924 to 1926.

**ILFORD** Ilford F.C. one of the last British teams to visit Germany before the First World War and the first team to travel there after the Armistice.

**LEICESTER** Venue of the first Amateur International match against Scotland in 1926.

**LONDON** The Football Association formed on October 26, 1863, at the Freemason's Tavern, Lincoln's Inn Fields, London, E.C.4.

**LUTON** Joe Payne scored ten goals for Luton Town against Bristol Rovers in 1936.

**MALVERN** A famous Public School where football has been played from earliest days.

**MANCHESTER** Officials and players of Manchester United F.C. were killed in air crash at Munich in February 1958 when returning from a European Cup Tie. Frank Swift, famous England goalkeeper was among the dead.

**NORWICH** King George VI opened present ground at Carrow Road in 1938.

**NOTTINGHAM** Notts County F.C., the oldest team in the Football League, was founded in 1862.

Whistles were used for the first time in 1878 on ground of Nottingham Forest.

**OXFORD** A special week for schoolboys was organized by The Football Association for several seasons after the Second World War.

**PORTLAND** Prince Albert (afterwards King George VI) played in a football match while serving in H. M. S. *Collingwood* in 1913.

**PORTSMOUTH** The present Portsmouth Club came into being in 1898 when it replaced the Artillery team stationed there at that time.

**PRESTON** The venue of the first Gentlemen *v* Players match in 1886.

**RAMSGATE** A football match is played on the Goodwin Sands off Ramsgate on Christmas Day every year.

**RUISLIP** Seven men were accused of playing football in 1576, causing an affray likely to result in homicide or serious accident.

**SEDGEFIELD** Shrove Tuesday football was played in the streets from noon throughout the afternoon. The farmers played the rest.

**SHEFFIELD** The longest surviving club, Sheffield F.C., formed in 1857, who are still direct members of The Football Association.

**SMALL HEATH** Now Birmingham City F.C., was the first Club to appoint a Director.

**SOUTHAMPTON** A schoolboy playing in an English Schools Shield match scored 17 of his teams 21 goals.

Southampton F.C. visited Argentina early this century.

**SOUTH BANK** The oldest amateur club in the north east, founded in 1878.

**SOUTHEND** The present club returned to its home at Roots Hall after a lapse of 35 years.

**STOCKPORT** Venue of the first Amateur International match against Wales in 1908.

**STOKE-ON-TRENT** The present club was one of the first teams to pay their players; the rate was half a crown per match ($12\frac{1}{2}$p).

**SUNDERLAND** Alf Common became the first player to be transferred for a fee of £1,000. He moved from Sunderland to Middlesbrough.

**TOTTENHAM** The present club played its first match against Arsenal in November 1887.

**TURTON** One of the first clubs to be formed in Lancashire – in 1872. Adopted the rules of the London F.A. in 1874.

**WAKEFIELD** A prison League was formed among prisoners in 1929.

**WEST BROMWICH** The present club was formed in 1879 by a group of cricketers.

**WOLVERHAMPTON** W. C. Rose, a goalkeeper of Wolverhampton Wanderers F.C. made the first attempt to form a Players' Union in 1893.

160